MODERN FISHING TACKLE

MODERN FISHING TACKLE

by **Vlad Evanoff**

NEW YORK: A. S. BARNES AND COMPANY, INC.
LONDON: THOMAS YOSELOFF LTD.

FOREWORD

For a long time the author of this book has felt that there was a need for a single volume reference book which covers the entire fishing tackle field. There have been books written on fresh-water fishing tackle and others on salt-water tackle. But this new book combines the two and gives the angler a single volume containing all the pertinent information on fresh and salt-water fishing tackle.

The main idea behind the book has been to cover all the basic equipment such as rods, reels, lines, lures, and accessories used in almost every kind of fresh and salt-water fishing. In other words, it answers the many questions asked by novice and experienced anglers when they want to buy a fishing outfit for a specific type or method of fishing. The angler who wants to try fly fishing for the first time will find all the information he needs to buy the best rod, reel, line, lures, and accessories. The salt-water angler who wants to try surf fishing will find all the information he needs on this type of tackle to make a wise selection.

Many notable advances have been made in the field of fishing tackle and accessories since World War II. We now have domestic and imported fishing tackle which far surpasses anything made before the war. This book covers all these improvements and innovations.

Naturally in trying to cover such a vast and complex field as fishing tackle there are bound to be some omissions. But the author feels that the average angler is interested in basic fishing tackle which will enable him to catch the fish he seeks. And in this book such an angler will find any tackle he needs for almost any kind of fresh or salt-water fishing. Properly consulted and wisely used, it can save him time and money in choosing a fishing outfit.

VLAD EVANOFF

ACKNOWLEDGEMENT

The author wishes to thank the many fishing tackle companies and other firms which supplied information and photos which helped in the writing of this book.

CONTENTS

1

FRESH-WATER SPINNING RODS

Spinning rods have come a long way since the first ones were imported and made in this country right after World War II. At that time you had a choice of only a few models, weights, lengths, and actions. Now the choice is so wide and varied that you can find a fresh-water spinning rod for almost any kind of fishing you have in mind.

When spinning was first introduced, split-bamboo rods were very common. Now they have almost disappeared from the market, although a few are still being made. The cheaper bamboo rods just couldn't compete with glass rods, and they vanished from the scene. But in the more expensive price range a good split-bamboo rod is still a fine fishing tool.

Ordinary bamboo rods will break more easily than glass and require more care such as drying and varnishing, and they often take a set (permanent bend) after being used for a long time. However, impregnated bamboo rods such as those made by the Charles F. Orvis Co. are waterproofed with Bakelite resin and are not affected by water, humidity, or heat. So if you buy a bamboo rod, get a high quality product. When it comes to bamboo rods, only the best is worth having. Even then, you'll have to baby it and take care of it more than you would a glass rod.

Most fresh-water spinning rods are made from hollow glass

13

or solid glass. The hollow or tubular glass rods are the most popular and best for fresh-water spinning. They combine ruggedness with light weight and have good action. Some rods are made from solid glass. These are very strong and often less expensive. Still other rods are made from both solid glass and hollow glass, with the butt sections of solid glass for power and the tip section of hollow glass. However, the solid glass rods are heavier, slower in action, and no match for hollow glass rods in over-all performance. Yet they make a good second rod for use in trolling and still fishing, where the strain or heavy sinkers may damage or break a light hollow glass rod. Many people also buy solid glass rods for youngsters who lack the experience to use a more delicate expensive rod.

Most of the reputable rod manufacturers make a good fresh-water spinning rod; but there are differences in the design, materials, and construction used. It all depends on the type of glass used, the kind of bonding agent, taper, diameter, and thickness of the glass blank. The cheaper rods are made from a cloth of coarser glass fibers or filaments, and fewer layers are used. The result is that the cheaper rod has less glass and more resin. The better rods, on the other hand, have finer glass fibers; and more layers are used with less resin or other bonding agent.

The better rods also have more expensive component parts or fittings such as ferrules, guides, reel seats, and handles. Ferrules on the better rods are usually made from nickel silver, stainless steel or anodized aluminum, or similar alloys. The cheaper rods usually have plated brass ferrules.

The type of reel seat or fastening used to hold the reel also varies with the manufacturer. More and more fresh-water spinning rods are being made with fixed locking reel seats similar to those that are used on salt-water rods. These have a screw thread and knurled ring which holds a spinning reel securely in place. Such fixed reel seats are made of light metals such as anodized aluminum on the light rods and of heavier stainless steel or plated brass metal on the heavier rods.

Originally most fresh-water spinning rods had two metal rings sliding on the cork handle to hold the reel in place. The rings are forced over the feet of the spinning reel to hold it firmly against the cork. This system works fine if the cork is new and there is a tight fit. But it tends to compress the cork handle and leave indentations. After a while the sliding metal rings may not hold the reel securely. One advantage of using the metal rings is that they allow the angler to change the position of his reel on the handle. However, very few anglers take advantage of this and use the reel in the same position most of the time. Today the sliding rings are used mostly on the lighter fresh-water spinning rods to cut down weight. Even then it's a good idea to use an adhesive or plastic tape over the rings to hold the reel more securely.

Still another system of holding the reel in place consists of a pair of rings around a movable metal or plastic shoe. There is a section cut out for the reel foot to fit into place. This type of reel seat also slides up and down on the reel handle and enables you to place the reel exactly where you want it.

The cork grip or handle on fresh-water spinning rods also varies in quality and construction. A cheap rod has cork which is soft and spongy or pitted. Other rods have handles or grips made of cork composition. But the most expensive rods usually have fine quality cork which is firm, free from pits, and glued together in a series of cork rings so tightly that it looks like one molded section. It also feels smooth and silky in your hand.

The guides on a fresh-water spinning rod are a small but important item. There should be enough guides to take the strain of casting and playing a fish along the entire length of the rod. The number of guides used varies according to the length and stiffness of the rod, but there should be at least five guides in addition to the tip-top. The guides should be properly spaced

to follow the curve of the rod. You can easily test this by string-
ing a line through the guides. Then tie the line to something or
have someone hold it, and then bend the rod. The line should
follow the curve of the rod closely and not touch the rod at any
point.

The guides should be made from some hard material such
as chrome-plated tungsten steel or Carboloy. Some rods also
have stainless steel guides, and these are good if the steel is hard.
A few spin rods are also made with genuine agate guides, which
are very hard. But they can be easily cracked by banging against
a hard object and must be replaced if broken.

Guides on most spinning rods graduate in size from a large
guide nearest the reel to smaller diameter ones toward the tip.
This is especially true with spinning rods used with open-face
or open-spool spinning reels. Here the line leaves the reel in
a wide circular or spiral motion which must be narrowed down.
The guides can be much smaller if used with closed-faced spinning reels.

The most common type of guide consists of a ring supported
by four legs fused to two feet which lay against the rod. Some of
the larger guides also have a bridge support attached to the ring
as added reinforcement. Another type of guide has a single
piece of wire twisted to form a ring and two legs. Still another
type has a ring which is cocked at an angle to form a funnel and
has only one foot instead of the usual two. This guide allows
more flexibility and also prevents the line from fouling around
it.

The windings which hold the guides on a spinning rod
should be tight and close together so that there are no spaces
between the threads. The windings and the rod should be var-
nished to protect the threads and the glass blank. Although
glass rods do not rot or deteriorate from moisture like split-
bamboo, it's still a good idea to varnish them. It not only im-

proves the appearance, but the extra coats of varnish protect the glass from ordinary scratches and scrapes.

The cheaper spinning rods come without bags or cases or with cloth bags. The more expensive rods have not only good quality heavy cloth bags but also fiber or aluminum cases. This protects the rod from breakage when transported or stored.

For the purpose of classification, we can divide fresh-water rods into four groups: ultra-light, light, medium, and heavy. In recent years ultra-light spinning has been growing in popularity, and now many rod manufacturers are making rods in this category. The ultra-light or UL rods range from $4\frac{1}{2}$ to 6 ft. in length and weigh from 1 to 3 oz. They are used with lines testing from $\frac{1}{2}$ lb. to 4 lb. to cast lures weighing from $\frac{1}{32}$ oz. to $\frac{1}{4}$ oz. Such a rod is used with the lightest fresh-water spinning reels. The whole outfit, rod and reel combined, may weigh only 7 or 8 oz. Such featherweight outfits are a pleasure to hold in your hand; and you can fish with them all day and not tire your wrist, not to mention the sport you obtain with the smallest trout, bass, and panfish. The ultra-light outfit is deadly when used for wary fish in low, clear, heavily fished waters.

Naturally there are limitations to the use of ultra-light tackle which must be observed. It is not an outfit for all-around fishing or for waters where there are any obstructions such as rocks, logs, weeds, sunken trees, etc. It is not the best rod to use where the fish run big or the current is very strong. And it is not the best outfit for a beginner since it takes considerable skill to fight and land fish on the hairlines used.

The light fresh-water spinning rods range from 6 to $7\frac{1}{2}$ ft. in length and weigh from $2\frac{1}{2}$ to $4\frac{1}{2}$ oz. They will cast lures weighing from $\frac{1}{8}$ to $\frac{3}{8}$ oz. and are used with lines testing 3 or 4 lb. Such a rod is best for trout, small or medium sized bass, pickerel, and panfish. It can be used to fish in streams and lakes where there aren't too many obstructions.

The medium fresh-water spinning rods are the nearest thing

to an all-around spinning outfit. This is the best rod for the beginner or for the angler who can buy only one rod. Such a medium rod will run from 6 to 7½ ft. in length and weigh from 4 to 6 oz. It can cast lures weighing from ¼ to ⅝ oz., which includes most of the spinning lures as well as many bait-casting lures. Lines testing 4 or 6 lb. are usually used with such a rod, but you can also use 8 lb. test lines for casting the heavier lures and in places where there are obstructions or big fish. The medium rod can be used for most of the fish found in fresh water such as big trout, black bass, walleyes, small pike, and big panfish. It can also be used for bait fishing with light sinkers for most of the fish above as well as for small bullheads or catfish, carp, suckers and any other small or medium sized freshwater fish.

The heavy fresh-water spinning rods range from 6½ to 9 ft. in length. They may weigh anywhere from 5 to 10 oz. and may be used with lines testing from 8 to 25 lb. The shorter and lighter rods can be cast with one hand, while the longer, heavier ones are for two-handed casting. Rods in the heavy fresh-water class are very similar to those used for light salt-water spinning. In fact, you can use many of these rods for both fresh and saltwater fishing. They will handle lures weighing from ½ to 2 oz., depending on the line used and action of the rod. The smaller one-handed rods are ideal for big black bass, pike, muskellunge, lake trout, salmon, and steelhead. However, many rods in this class are called "salmon-steelhead" rods and are extra long for two-handed casting in the Pacific Northwest for these fish. The heavy fresh-water spinning rods can also be used for fishing in strong currents and waters filled with obstructions where light tackle is impractical. Heavy rods also make good tools for fishing on the bottom with heavy sinkers for fish such as big catfish and carp.

The length of the rod you buy for fresh-water spinning will depend on your own personal preference and the type of fishing you do. Most spinning rods are made in 6, 6½, and 7 ft. lengths, with the 6½ the most popular. Since such length rods are available in the light, medium, or heavy classes, you rarely need a shorter or a longer rod. Of course, ultra-light rods are usually shorter; and for casting natural baits more delicately, you may need a longer rod. But most of the all-purpose fresh-water spinning rods will fall in the 6 to 7 ft. range.

While some fresh-water spinning rods are made in one piece, the great majority are made in two pieces with the ferrule in the middle breaking the rod into two equal lengths or exactly in half. This is most convenient for transporting since such a rod will fit into a rigid fiber, plastic, or metal case. You can also get three and four-piece rods which break down into short lengths for easy packing in a suitcase or other small space.

The kind of "action" a spinning rod has is important because it will determine the distance and accuracy of your casts. Some spinning rods are made with what is called a fast tip action. Only a short section of the tip of the rod bends or flexes when a lure is cast. Such rods are difficult to cast with and are not very satisfactory for playing a fish. You'll also have trouble casting light lures with such a rod. The spinning rods with a greater bending length are easier to cast with, handle the lighter lures better, and are more satisfactory for playing fish. However, most rods with the regular actions are limited to a certain range of lure weights.

The progressive taper action rods, on the other hand, have been developed to handle a wide range of lures. If you use light lures, only the extreme sensitive tip section will bend when casting. If you change to a heavier lure, more of the rod is brought into play; and it bends farther down toward the butt. Then if you change to a still heavier lure, the full length of the rod is brought into play; and it curves almost to the butt. With such an action in a spinning rod, you can handle a much wider range of lures than with other rods. Such a rod is ideal for the man who is getting only one fresh-water spinning rod. It costs somewhat more than other rods, but its versatility in handling different lure weights makes it the nearest thing to an "all-around" rod made today.

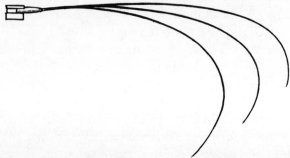

Bends taken by a progressive taper rod under the pull of different weights

But no matter what kind of action you seek, try to avoid rods which are soft, sloppy, and which have excessive vibration. One test which can be made in a tackle store is to hold the rod butt against your stomach with the tip pointing out in front of you. Hold both hands on the cork handle firmly. Then slowly waggle the rod back and forth from left to right until you see the rod bending as far down the tip as possible. Then stop the movement abruptly. The rod should stop vibrating almost immediately. If it continues to vibrate for some time after you stop it, forget about it. You won't get much accuracy or distance with such a rod.

The regular spinning rods covered here can be used with both the open-face spinning reels and the closed-faced types which hang under the rod handle.

Fresh-water spinning rods vary in price from a few dollars up to $70.00 or more for the finer glass and split-bamboo models. It is best to avoid the cheapest rods and get one in the $15.00 to $35.00 range to insure good quality parts and workmanship.

2

FRESH-WATER SPINNING REELS

The growth in the popularity of spinning in this country is amazing when you realize that it all happened since World War II. Before the War bait-casting tackle was the most popular for fresh-water fishing. But it took a century or more for bait-casting to reach the same popularity as spinning now enjoys.

Of course, spinning reels as such took more than fifty years to reach their present stage of development. An Englishman named Alfred Holden Illingworth made the first true workable spinning reel based on the fixed spool principle in 1905. The reel became popular and spread to France, Switzerland, Italy, and other parts of Europe.

Spinning was first introduced to America by Bache Brown, who started to import spin reels as early as 1935. He gave demonstrations at sports shows and started to market the reels. Just as they were beginning to catch on, World War II came along and put a stop to the whole business.

But after the War, in 1946, renewed interest in spinning began to take shape; and spinning reels and rods were imported from Europe. Besides Bache Brown, Joseph Bates and George Thommen and a few others also played a big part in popularizing spinning in the United States through demonstrations, books, and magazine articles. Anglers became curious, tried spinning, liked it, and the rush was on. It wasn't long before foreign and American manufacturers started flooding the market with imported and domestic spinning reels.

The advantages of spinning reels over other types are so well known by now that almost every angler or prospective angler is familiar with them. The most important contribution of the spinning reel has been the elimination of the dreaded "backlash" or "bird's nest," which troubled anglers using revolving spool reels for over a hundred years.

The basic difference between a spinning reel and a conventional revolving spool reel is that the spin reel has a stationary or "fixed" spool which doesn't revolve during a cast. The conventional bait-casting reel has a revolving spool which turns as the line leaves the reel during a cast. This spool must be controlled with the thumb or some sort of gadget which keeps it turning at the proper speed. If it goes too fast, the line doesn't leave the spool to keep pace; and a bad tangle or backlash results. If the spool slows down too much, you don't get any distance. A revolving spool needs a fairly heavy lure or weight to overcome the inertia of the spool and line and start it moving, so obtaining any distance with light lures with a revolving spool reel is difficult.

The spinning reel, on the other hand, has no revolving spool. The line leaves the stationary spool freely and just coils off without any movement of the reel parts. You don't have to use your thumb or fingers to control the cast. The line spills off as long as the lure or weight exerts a pull. The minute the lure hits the water, the line stops moving off the reel spool. It's so simple that you can cast a surprising distance on the very first attempts.

Since there is no revolving spool which must be started moving by the lure or weight, the line on a spinning reel requires very little pull to get it going. A tiny, light lure or weight will start the line peeling off the reel spool. This, of course, means that spinning anglers are free from those pesky back-lashes and that they can cast the lightest lures. These are two big advantages they have over the anglers using the revolving bait-casting reels.

There are basically three types of spinning reels which work on the fixed-spool principle. The first is the open-faced or open-spool spinning reel. The second is the closed-faced spinning reel, which mounts under the rod. And the third is the "spin-casting" or "push-button" reel, which mounts above the rod. In this chapter we are concerned mainly with the open-faced and closed-faced reels which hang below the rod. The following chapter will cover the spin-cast reels.

The open-faced spinning reel, as the name implies, has the spool exposed so that you can see the line. This reel was developed first, and it wasn't until much later that the closed-faced type reels came along.

An important part of any open-faced spinning reel is the line pick-up, which catches the line and then winds it back on the reel spool after a cast. The earlier spinning reels had a "manual" pick-up, and some spinning reels with such pick-ups are still being made today. Here the angler uses his index finger on the right hand to catch the line after a cast, then guides it back to where the manual pick-up roller engages the line, and then winds it back on the reel. This method is the most fool-proof of all, and some anglers like it best. After practice the movements become automatic, and the line is picked up with little trouble. One big advantage of the manual pick-up is that it results in a somewhat sturdier reel with fewer delicate parts to get out of order or wear out. There are also fewer places for the line to tangle.

Another type of pick-up is the finger or arm type, which was commonly found on earlier models. Quite a few salt-water reels are still made with this type of pick-up, but it is becoming less popular for fresh-water fishing. This pick-up has a short, curved finger or arm which swings into position and catches the line for winding back on the reel spool. This is automatic and just requires turning of the reel handle to pick up the line. One disadvantage of the arm pick-up is that on some reels it often misses the line, and sometimes the line tangles around the arm. And the pick-up arms or fingers are often bent out of shape if they are not made of thick stock.

The most common type of pick-up found on the majority of fresh and salt-water reels is the third type. This is called the "full-bail" pick-up. Here you have a wire hoop which catches the line and throws or slides it into the groove or roller when the reel handle is turned. This is automatic, and a spinning reel with a good working bail is very convenient to use. Expert anglers like it because it is fast working and is especially handy when fishing with artificial lures, which must be reeled back the instant they hit the water. Beginners like the bail pick-up because it is easy to use and requires little practice.

Many spinning reels with bail pick-ups can also be converted to manual in a short time. This is usually done by removing the bail and adding a conversion unit or stud, which is sold at a modest price. A few reels can be used manually simply by removing the bail. Such reels offer the advantage that if anything goes wrong with the bail, you can continue fishing with the reel by changing to manual operation.

The open-faced reels have a groove or roller over which the line runs when it is reeled back. This part takes a lot of wear when retrieving lures or fighting a big fish. It should be made of some hard substance such as sapphire, agate, or the hardest metal. If the roller is supposed to turn, it should do so freely. Otherwise a groove may appear where the line rubs against it.

The friction clutch or drag on a spinning reel is a very important part and performs a vital function. This is a mechanical device which enables the fish to take line out only under a steady tension. This, of course, permits the angler to fight the fish more easily and tire it out sooner. Drags vary somewhat in construction; but the majority make use of some sort of slipping clutch, which exerts pressure on the reel spool. These drags can be adjusted so that the amount of pressure on the spool can be regulated. On most reels this consists of a wing nut in front of the spool which can be tightened or loosened. But other reels have various devices at different parts of the reel for controlling the drag. On the well-known Swiss-made Record Reels, for example, the drag is regulated by turning a cup at the rear of the reel.

Because of the light lines used in fresh-water spinning, the drag is an important factor in handling and landing big fish. When a fish wants to run, a good drag enables him to do this without placing too much strain on the line or rod. So it pays to choose a reel with a drag that is smooth and efficient. And it should keep the tension at which it has been set. An imperfect drag may not matter when you use the heavier lines, but for light line spinning and for active fish which run and leap, the drag should be smooth with no jerking or binding.

The drag should also have a gradual adjustment instead of a sudden one. In other words, when you increase or decrease the drag, you should be able to do it a little at a time. On some reels a slight twist of the knob will increase the drag too much. If you do this during a fight with a fish, you may break the line.

The setting you use and how you set the drag is a controversial subject, and personal preferences enter into the picture. Some like to fish with a light drag, while others prefer as much drag as the line will take. Many anglers can pull the line off the reel and can tell by the feel of the tension if the drag is set right. This comes with experience, however, and for a beginner the most dependable method is to rig up your rod and reel and pull the line through the guides. Then get someone to run off about 75 ft. of line. If you are alone, you can tie the end of the line to a tree, post, or other solid support and then back up and let out line. Now tighten the drag slightly and back up. Keep backing up and tightening the drag until the rod takes its maximum bend. When it does bend almost as far as it will go, try backing up again. The line should slip off the reel spool not too easily or too tightly. This is about the maximum fishing drag for that particular line and rod, allowing for a safety margin.

For small fresh-water fish such as panfish, the drag can be set at this maximum and left that way. But if you are fishing for active gamefish which make long runs or leap, you can loosen the drag a bit more.

Many expert anglers claim that once the drag is set it should be left that way. This may hold true most of the time, but there are times when loosening or tightening a drag may be necessary. For example, if a fish like a steelhead or salmon makes a long run and you can't follow him, you may have to tighten the drag slightly to slow him down or try to prevent the fish from going out of the pool into the rapids. Or if a big fish heads for some weeds, rocks, or a sunken tree, you may also have to tighten the drag to try to turn him or at least slow him down. If a big fish makes a very long run, taking more than half the line off the spool, it may even be necessary to loosen the drag to take the strain off the line. However, this rarely occurs in fresh-water fishing and is more likely to happen in salt-water spin fishing for big fish.

When a fish is licked and turns over on its side near the boat or shore, it may be necessary to tighten the drag in order to bring it close enough for netting or beaching. This is especially true in rivers or streams where the current is swift and strong.

It isn't always necessary to tighten the drag by turning the knob or lever. You can exert pressure on the spool with your forefinger against the lip or flange. During a fight this is usually the best and safest way to add more drag pressure.

After some experience you get the feel of the spool and know just how hard you can press with your finger without breaking the line. If you use ultra-light tackle, you'll have to depend on finger pressure instead of the drag on the reel. No matter how smooth the drag is, it is impossible to set it properly for all the situations which may arise during a fight with a fish. So most ultra-light anglers set the drag very light and apply finger pressure as needed.

Most spinning reels also have an anti-reverse lock. When this is in the "on" position, it prevents the handle from turning backwards. Some fishermen leave it in the "on" position all the time so that they are ready if a fish is hooked. There's nothing wrong with this except that most spinning reels have a loud click when the anti-reverse is on, and this may be annoying. Other anglers fish with the anti-reverse in the "off" position and put it on soon after a fish is hooked. Some reels also have an automatic anti-reverse which takes over by itself.

The anti-reverse is especially useful when you are fishing alone and want to boat or land a fish. Then you can take your hand off the reel handle and use it for gaffing or netting a fish. The anti-reverse is also used when trolling or still fishing. Here you often put the rod down, and with the anti-reverse in the "on" position any strike is against the drag. And the audible click on the reel warns of a bite or strike.

The anti-reverse is also used when you are not fishing to prevent the handle from turning and loose line from spilling off the spool when the lure or hook gets caught on something.

You rarely have to worry about spool sizes or capacities. Most open-faced spinning reels carry more than enough line for average fishing conditions. Most fresh-water spinning reels will hold anywhere from 150 to 300 yd. of line depending on the size of the spool and the diameter of the line. Naturally, you can get more yards of 4 lb. test on the same reel than you can of 8 lb. test.

More important than the line capacity is an extra spool or two. These can be filled with different sized lines. The spool on the reel can have 4 lb. test, and the other spool can carry 6 lb. test. If you have a third spool, this can be filled with 8 lb. test for bigger fish or for fishing in strong currents or around obstructions. The spools on most open-faced spinning reels can usually be changed quickly.

The size and weight of the reel itself will vary depending on the materials used and the manufacturer. Most fresh-water open-faced reels range from 4 to 12 oz. in weight. The lightest ones are usually made of nylon, plastic, or similar materials. Or the reels are made very small for ultra-light fishing, also cutting down on the weight. If you go in for ultra-light fishing, you can find several small reels from which to choose. Two of the first reels to appear on the market were the Alcedo Micron, distributed by Continental Arms Co., and the Mignon 33, imported by the Rockland Tackle Co. The Garcia Corporation came out with their Mitchell 308 for what they call "Ultra Sports" fishing. These small reels range from about 5 to 8 oz. in weight and are made to match the featherweight rods and hairlines with which they are used. However, ultra-light tackle is best for the more advanced or experienced angler. For the beginner, the somewhat larger regular sized open-faced reels are better, especially if you want only one spinning reel for "all-around" fishing. Then you can use it with heavier lines and lures when needed.

For heavy-duty fresh-water spinning you may need a larger fresh-water spinning reel or a smaller salt-water model. Only rarely is a big salt-water spinning reel needed in fresh water. However, if you seek big catfish or sturgeon where lines testing 20 or 30 lb. will be used, then a big salt-water spinning reel may be necessary.

The closed spool or "American" type of reel was developed in this country. When the first open-faced reels appeared, some manufacturers felt that this reel could be improved or at least simplified. The result was the closed-faced spinning reel, which hangs below the rod. This was followed by the spin-casting reel, which is mounted above the rod.

The open-spool reel, of course, has the spool exposed; and the line spirals off in coils. In the closed-spool type, the spool is covered entirely or partially by a cover, usually cone or cupped shaped, which hides the spool. The line comes out of a hole in front of the cone. The open-faced reels require larger guides on the spinning rod, whereas the closed-faced reel casts well with smaller guides.

Another big difference between the two is that the closed faced reels do not use exposed line pick-ups such as bails or arms. Instead they generally have some kind of internal pick-up pin which moves out of the way when the cast is being made. Then, when the reel handle is turned, the pin emerges and catches the line to wind it back on the spool. The principle of casting is the same as with the open-spool reel since the spool doesn't revolve on the cast. So you can cast just as easily with the closed-type reels as with the open type with no backlashes.

The closed-type reels also have drags which can be adjusted for playing a fish. Most of them have smooth drags which do a good job on most fresh-water fish.

The closed-faced reels we are interested in here are those which hang below the rod like the open-faced reels. They usually come with the handle or crank on the left-hand side. You cast with your right hand and reel in with your left. However, you can also obtain such reels with handles on the right side for right-handed cranking.

Which reels are better—the closed spool or open spool? Well, it all depends on the angler and the type of fishing he plans to do. When closed-faced reels first came out, they had some defects such as the line binding on the narrow spool or twisting badly on the retrieve or being pinched or ruined by some part of the reel. These reels have been improved greatly in recent years, however, and are practical, efficient fishing tools.

The main disadvantage of a closed-spool reel is that you can't cast very light lures as far with it as with an open-faced reel. And you can't use very light lines on closed-faced reels. It also takes a bit more time to change spools on a closed-type reel. For the ultra-light or light spinning specialist, the open-faced spinning reel is best.

However, the closed-faced reels are simple, durable, and almost foolproof. They are easier and simpler to operate with fewer manual motions to master or remember. So for the average angler or beginner who doesn't spend much time fishing or practice casting, these reels are ideal.

Casting with the one-handed fresh-water spinning rod and open-faced reel is done with the right hand holding the rod directly above the reel. The thumb rests on top of the cork handle while two fingers are below in front of the reel leg and the other two fingers are behind this support. However, this may vary with the angler. Some like to place three fingers in front of the reel leg or foot. In some closed-faced reels the

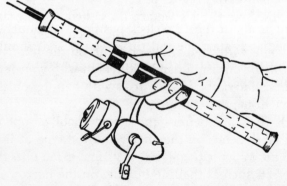

Holding spinning rod and open-faced spinning reel

whole hand is in front of the reel. Follow the instruction booklet enclosed with the reel for clarification of this point.

The basic spinning cast is the overhead cast. The lure or
casting weight should hang about 6 in. from the tip of the rod.
The first step is to move the pick-up device into casting position. With a manual-type reel you bring the line roller to the
top so that you can pick up the line with the index finger of
your right hand. Then the line roller is moved out of the way
so that it rests at the bottom of the reel.

With reels having finger or arm pick-ups you do the same
thing, turning the handle so that the line can be grabbed with
the index finger. Back away the handle so that the pick-up
moves to the bottom of the reel, and then push the finger or
arm away from the reel spool.

When using the full-bail pick-up reel, you turn the handle
until the line roller is on top permitting you to grab the line
with your index finger. Then back off the reel handle so that
the line is free from the roller. Finally, using your left hand,
push the wire bail down until it is in casting position at the
bottom of the reel.

When your reel is ready to cast, rest the line on the ball of
your index finger. Next hold the rod at about the 10 o'clock
position in front of you. Point it at the target. Now bring the
rod back fast toward you so that the tip points into the air above
your head at about the 12 o'clock position. Without waiting,
you immediately start the rod tip forward. This should be a
fast, snappy movement. As the rod moves forward it will bend
into an arc under the weight of the lure. When it reaches the
10 o'clock position again, the index finger releases the line,
and the lure will shoot out in front of you. When it reaches
the target or just above it, you drop your finger to the lip of the
spool to stop the cast. You can also stop the cast by turning the
handle on an automatic finger or bail pick-up reel.

If your lure goes up high into the air, it means that you

released the line too soon. If it drops at your feet or a short distance away, it means you released the line too late. It will take a little practice before you get the timing just right.

This is the basic overhead cast. Once you learn this well, the other casts will be easy. The overhead cast is the most accurate and will drop your lure in a straight line in front of you. In actual fishing, however, where the lure doesn't have to hit a small target, the rod is held a bit to the right side.

In the side cast the rod travels almost parallel to the ground or water. It is not as accurate as the overhead cast but is useful for casting under overhanging trees or into a strong wind. The lure travels low, and you get more distance against the wind.

Another cast which will enable you to fish from shore in heavy brush and woods is the bow-and-arrow cast. Here you let the lure hang down about half the length of the rod. Then you grab the lure carefully with your left fingers at the bend of the hook (not ahead of the points) and pull back until the rod flexes into a bow. The rod can bend up or down; it doesn't make much difference. Now aim toward the target. Then release the lure with your left hand, and let the line slip off your index finger.

Another cast used in heavy brush is the lariat or circle cast. Here the lure dangles from the rod tip about a foot or so, and you twirl it around in a circle in front of you. When it reaches a good speed, you release the line, and the lure shoots out to one side. To cast in the opposite direction, you twirl the rod in the other direction.

There are a few other casts, but the ones above will take care of most of your fishing situations. You'll pick up others as you go along. In the beginning it pays to try for accuracy and not distance. After you learn how to cast, you can increase your distance.

When casting with closed-spool type reels, you go through the same motions as above. The only thing that may be different is the release of the line, depending on the model of the reel you are using. With some of them you hold the line on your index finger the same as with open-faced spinning reels. But with others you hold the line against the cork handle, then let it go. Still others like the Zebco reel have a trigger which releases the line. Study the instruction sheet or booklet which comes with the reel for further details.

3

SPIN-CASTING RODS AND REELS

Although the open and closed-faced spinning reels are extremely popular, they are being challenged by the so-called "spin-cast" or "push-button" type reels. These are the closed-faced reels which are mounted above the rod like a bait-casting reel. To cast with them you simply push a button, begin your cast, then release the button to start the lure on its way. These reels are so easy to use that they have zoomed in popularity, and in many parts of the country they are outselling all other types of fresh-water reels.

The spin-casting reel is almost foolproof, and you rarely have trouble with the line tangling or uncoiling as sometimes happens with the open-faced spinning reels. This is especially desirable when fishing on a windy day or at night. The spin-cast reel is also more accurate and faster to use than the open-faced reel. You can time the release of your lure to a split second when casting and send it flying to the target with precision and speed.

The main disadvantage of the spin-casting reel is that it won't cast quite as far, especially with light lures. And you have to use at least a 4 lb. test with such reels. Most of them use a 6 or 8 lb. test line, so it isn't the reel for the fresh-water angler who wants to use ultra-light lures and lines. If you fish in waters where extremely long casts are required, you're better off with an open-faced spinning reel. But for the average man, woman, or child who doesn't fish too much or too often, it's ideal for all-around fresh-water fishing.

Another big advantage of the spin-cast reel is that you can use it with a bait-casting rod that you already have instead of going out and buying a special rod. However, some bait-casting rods may be too stiff or too short to do a good job with a spin-casting reel. So you would be better off buying a lighter or more limber rod or one of the special "spin-casting" rods. More and more manufacturers are making such rods for use with both spin-casting and bait-casting reels. Other rod manufacturers make both types of rods.

The main differences between a spin-casting rod and a bait-casting rod are the length, action, and type and size of the guides. In general the bait-casting rods are somewhat shorter, stiffer in action, and have smaller guides. In comparison, spin-casting rods are longer, have a more limber tip action, and have larger guides.

Spin-casting rods are made in various types of actions and lengths. Some rod manufacturers list four different actions: extra-light, light, medium, and heavy. Others make the spin-casting rods in only two or three actions. Although some of the light action spin-rods used with a 4 lb. test line can cast a $\frac{1}{8}$ oz. lure a fair distance, and the heavy action rods can handle lures up to one ounce, most spin-casting rods are made to handle lures in the $\frac{1}{4}$ to $\frac{5}{8}$ oz. range.

The length of the spin-casting rod you use will depend on your personal preference. Most of them come in 6, $6\frac{1}{2}$, and 7 ft. over-all lengths although one company, Wright & McGill, recently came out with a so-called "Special Duty" rod which has an offset reel seat to accommodate spin-casting reels. This rod is 8 ft. in over-all length and has an extra long 10 inch butt, grip, or handle. It can be cast with two hands if needed and is recommended for heavy fresh-water fishing such as bait fishing, trolling, and drift fishing for steelhead and salmon.

But for most of your fishing a 6 or 6½ ft. spin-casting rod will be adequate. Such rods are usually made in two sections with a ferrule in the middle. But they can also be obtained in three pieces with a detachable handle and two section tip. Other spin-casting rods are made with long one-piece tips and detachable handles. Still other special spin-casting rods are made in four sections for easy packing in a small space.

The reel seat on most spin-casting rods is the same offset type found on most bait-casting rods. These seats are usually made from die-cast aluminum or other metals and plastics. The reel seat on such rods should lock a spin-casting reel securely in place. The grips and handles are made of cork or plastic.

The guides on a spin-casting rod are smaller than those found on rods used with open-faced spinning reels, but they are somewhat larger than those found on a true bait-casting rod. However, as stated before, many manufacturers are now making the same rod for use with both spin-casting and bait-casting reels. Therefore the size of the guides used will work well with either type of reel.

The great majority of spin-casting rods are made from hollow or tubular glass blanks. These have the best action for all-around spin-casting. Some of the cheapest rods are made from solid glass; and while inferior in action and heavier than hollow glass, such rods are extremely strong and are suitable for rough fishing or youngsters.

The closed-faced spin-casting reel is very similar to the closed-faced spinning reel covered in the last chapter. But instead of hanging below the rod like the other spinning reels, the spin-cast reel is mounted above the rod. However, the construction and mechanical operation of the spin-cast reel is similar to the type which hangs below the rod.

The spin-cast reel also has a cone-shaped face in front of the reel. The line comes out of a small hole and loses most of its swirl, thus enabling this reel to be used with rods having small guides. The hole through which the line comes out is lined with a smooth, hard metal ring so that the line doesn't wear. The cone in front of the reel can usually be removed quickly and easily on most of the reels for quick access to the line on the spool.

Most of the spin-casting reels also have a thumb button or trigger, which is pushed and held down when ready to cast. Then, when the lure is released, the thumb is lifted off the button. On many of the reels you can also press on the button lightly, feathering it while the lure is in flight to control or slow down its speed. To stop the cast you can press down firmly on the button.

Spin-casting reels also have an anti-reverse, which prevents the handle from turning backwards. On some reels this consists of a knurled ring or button which can be turned to the "on" or "off" position as required. But many other spin-cast reels are made with a permanent anti-reverse which stays on at all times.

The brakes or drags found on most spin-casting reels are generally smooth and efficient. When they first appeared, some of the earlier models were troublesome in this respect. The drag would be uneven, or the line would bind and would break. Different makes have different types of drags and methods of drag adjustment. Most of the spin-casting reels have a knob or lever which is moved to increase or decrease the drag tension. Some are numbered from 0 to 8 or higher so that the drag can be set at a predetermined tension. Other reels have star-drags such as those found on conventional salt-water reels.

The spools on most spin-casting reels are much narrower than those found on open-faced spinning reels. This solves the problem of the lines piling up unevenly in the front or back of the spool as often happens with the wider open-faced spinning reels. However, the narrow spool also creates another problem in some reels by causing the parallel wound line to bury itself under the other strands of line under tension such as when the angler is playing a fish or pulling on the line when he gets fouled or caught. This buried line must be worked free before another cast can be made. This problem has been remedied in later models, which cross-wind the line to overcome this tendency.

The line pick-up pin which catches the line during the retrieve should be made of some hard substance such as Carboloy. There is a lot of wear and friction at this point, and a soft metal will become grooved and eventually damage the line. Some of the earlier models of spin-casting reels also twisted the line badly when it was rewound on the spool. This twisting has been eliminated on many of the later models.

Most spin-casting reels have interchangeable spools which can be removed and replaced by other spools filled with new line or lines of different tests. Most of the spin-casting reels come filled with 6 or 8 lb. test monofilament line from the factory. Some fresh-water models can also be used with lines testing 10, 12, or 15 lb. There are also a few special heavy duty fresh-water and salt-water spin-casting reels which can be used with heavier lines up to 20 lb. test or so. For most fresh-water fishing, lines testing 6 or 8 lb. test are sufficient. The average spin-casting reel will hold anywhere from 80 to 150 yd. of line, depending on the pound test; and this is more than enough for fresh-water fishing.

Spin-casting reels are usually made of light metals such as aluminum alloys which are anodized or satin-chromed to protect them. However, more and more plastics are being utilized in making such reels. The Zebco Co. is now using "Delrin"— an acetal resin plastic by Du Pont which is claimed to be "salt-water proof." Its properties of rigidity, toughness, and resiliency result in a lightweight, durable reel which is supposed to require almost no maintenance.

The majority of spin-casting reels are made with a right-hand crank or handle. In other words, you're supposed to cast with your right hand, then transfer the rod and reel to your left hand to turn the reel handle with your right hand. However, some companies also make spin-casting reels with a left-hand crank for retrieving with your left hand, like most open-faced spinning reels. Other spin-casting reels can be changed so that the handle is either on the left or right-hand side. Whichever reel you get depends on your own habits and personal preference. If you have used a bait-casting or surf-casting conventional revolving spool reel most of your life, you'll find the right-hand crank most familiar. If you started fishing with an open-faced spinning reel, then you'll probably find the left-hand crank the most familiar. That way you don't have to learn or unlearn any hand movements. But it really doesn't take very long to get used to a new reel if you cast and fish with it often enough.

Casting with a spin-casting reel is so easy and simple that it

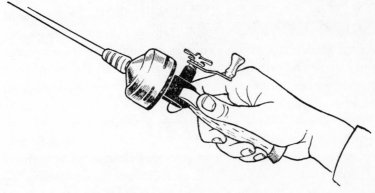

Holding spin-casting rod and reel

requires hardly any detailed explanation. The clerk in any fishing tackle store will show you the operation of the reel and rod and hand movements, and then you're all set. Here's a brief rundown of the procedure: Hold the rod so that the reel handle faces up and point it at the target. Press the thumb button and hold it down to lock the line and lure in place. The lure should hang about 3 to 6 in. from the rod tip. Now bring the rod back sharply to the 12 o'clock position, directly over your head. Then start the forward cast almost immediately and release the button so that the line is freed and the lure can sail out. On most spin-casting reels you can stop the cast by pressing the button. Then you simply turn the handle forward to catch the line again so that it can be retrieved.

The spin-casting reel has made it so simple to cast that instead of spending hours, days, or weeks practicing how to cast you can go out on the first day and concentrate on catching fish instead of worrying if you can cast far enough. Of course, even with a spin-casting reel you must do quite a bit of casting until you can place the lure on a dime. But in most waters such accuracy is not required; and if the lure or bait lands a few feet from the target, it usually doesn't make too much difference in open waters. Spin-casting reels are so easy to use and so foolproof that even expert anglers like to use them at night, when other reels are apt to give trouble.

4

BAIT CASTING RODS AND REELS

Before spinning tackle was introduced into the United States, most fresh-water anglers used bait-casting tackle. In fact, for over a century the bait-casting rod and reel reigned supreme as the method of taking warm-water fish, especially black bass. This type of angling originated in this country, dating back to the early 1800's when a Kentucky watchmaker named George Snyder invented the first multiplying reel. This reel was geared so that it made almost four revolutions of the spool to each turn of the reel handle. This not only enabled the angler to retrieve his line and lures much faster but also produced a reel which cast much easier and smoother than earlier models.

As the popularity of spinning grew, the interest in bait-casting waned; and many novice and casual anglers have never used a bait-casting reel. Today most newcomers to fresh-water fishing start off with spinning tackle, and the majority stay with such gear. Most of the bait-casting outfits being used today are used by old-time anglers who started with casting rods and reels and continue to use them or by expert anglers who alternate between fly fishing, bait-casting, and spinning.

But even though more fresh-water anglers use spinning or spin-casting outfits than bait-casting, there are definite places and fishing conditions where the older method is superior. In the hands of a skilled angler the bait-casting outfit provides pinpoint accuracy. He can drop his lure into a smaller area alongside lily pads, hyacinths, logs, stumps, and near shore or under overhanging trees with less danger of hanging up. And even if he does hang up, he can often break loose without losing his lure. If you hook a big fish near such obstructions, you can use more force and pressure to get him away from there in a hurry. With spinning or fly tackle it is more difficult to stop or turn a big fish. Bait-casting tackle is also better for casting and using the heavier fresh-water lures. It not only casts them better but sets the hooks into the tough mouth of big fish more easily. And if you fish deep with bottom bouncing lures where you hang up often or hook big fish, you'll find the bait-casting outfit more practical. You'll have fewer break-offs and lose fewer lures and big fish. Besides, there's a certain feel to a bait-casting reel with your thumb on the line which is lacking a spinning or spin-casting reel. This enables expert anglers to manipulate their lures more effectively, detect more strikes, and play a big fish with a quicker, surer adjustment of tension on the line.

Because of these advantages you'll find many anglers in the deep South still using bait-casting outfits for black bass. The cypress stumps and trees, roots, lily pads, and hyacinths choke many bass waters in Florida, Georgia, Mississippi, Alabama, and Louisiana. So the man with a sturdy bait-casting rod and reel has a definite advantage over a man with a spinning outfit. Bait-casting outfits also have a popularity among many anglers in the Pacific Northwest among steelhead and salmon anglers. And they are widely used by many anglers going after pike, muskies and lake trout in our northern states and Canada.

The main disadvantage of bait-casting tackle is that it's not as simple to use as spinning or even fly-casting tackle. It calls for more practice and know-how in casting, working the lures, and fighting a fish than these other kinds. So the "once-in-a-blue moon" angler who gets little chance to go fishing or practice with bait-casting tackle is better off with spinning tackle. And the beginner who won't practice casting will also do better with spin-casting or spinning tackle. Finally, the average bait-casting outfit can't cast light lures as efficiently as a spinning outfit. And you can't use bait-casting tackle when fish are taking tiny flies off the surface of the water. A fly fishing outfit is supreme under such conditions.

However, the skill and know-how involved in using a bait-casting outfit gives great satisfaction to its users, so many anglers take up the challenge offered by bait-casting and use it as often as they can when it fits the fishing conditions.

There is no such thing as an all-around or single bait-casting outfit to cast all weights of lures or for all fishing conditions. You have to decide in advance the weight of the lures you will cast, where you will fish, and the average size of the fish which will be caught. Then you can choose a bait-casting outfit which will come closest to suiting your needs.

You can separate most bait-casting outfits into three classes: light, medium, and heavy. The light outfit will have a rod going from $5\frac{1}{2}$ to 6 ft. in length with a limber action. The reel will be a small, narrow spool type filled with line going from 6 to 10 lb. Such an outfit will cast lures weighing from $\frac{1}{4}$ to $\frac{1}{2}$ oz. best. Such an outfit is also best for small or medium-sized fish such as black bass, big trout, pickerel, and panfish and for clear water and wary fish. It should be used mostly in open waters free from obstructions.

The medium bait-casting outfit has a rod going anywhere from 4 to 6 ft. It can be used with a narrow spool or regular width reel filled with line testing anywhere from 10 to 18 lb. Such an outfit casts best with lures going from $\frac{1}{2}$ to $\frac{3}{4}$ oz. The typical $\frac{5}{8}$ oz. lures made for bait-casting are all handled nicely with this outfit. This is the nearest thing to an all-around casting rig for fresh water. If you can only get one bait-casting outfit, this is the one to get for black bass, walleyes, pike, and muskies. It can also be used in salt water for many kinds of fish.

The heavy bait-casting outfit has a rod going from 4 to 7 ft. with fairly stiff action. A standard width bait-casting reel with or without free spool or star-drag can be used with this rod. The line will test anywhere from 18 to 25 lb. Lures weighing from ¾ to 1½ oz. can be handled with this outfit. Such a rod and reel can be used for big black bass in snag-filled waters and for pike, muskies, steelhead, Pacific salmon, and lake trout. It can also be used for bait fishing for the larger fresh-water fish such as carp and catfish or in salt waters for striped bass, snook, weakfish, tarpon, and other species.

There is also the extra-light or ultra-light bait-casting outfit which has a rod going 6 to 6½ ft. in length. It is used with a tournament type or narrow spool reel filled with a line testing from 4 to 8 lb. It can be used to cast lures weighing from about ⅛ to ⅜ oz. Such an outfit is used mostly by a small number of expert anglers for big trout, black bass, and other fresh-water fish. However, for casting the lightest lures, most anglers are much better off with a spinning outfit.

Choosing a bait-casting rod these days isn't too difficult when it comes to getting a good quality, serviceable rod. Most of the rods made by reputable manufacturers will prove satisfactory. It need not be expensive, for a bait-casting rod costing $10.00 or $12.00 will do as good a job of casting as one costing twice as much.

The early bait-casting rods ran up to 8 feet in length and were usually made from a solid wood such as hickory, betha-bara, lancewood, and other woods. Then they were made from bamboo and solid or tubular steel. Split bamboo and tubular steel rods reached a high popularity until glass rods came along. Some split bamboo and metal rods are still to be seen, but they have largely been replaced by solid and hollow glass bait-casting rods.

A solid glass rod is very strong and can take a surprising amount of abuse before breaking. It casts well enough for most purposes and is a good rod for a young child as as an extra bait-casting rod for trolling or bait-fishing with a heavy sinker. However, solid glass rods are only a few dollars cheaper than good hollow glass rods; so if you are buying your first bait-casting rod, you can't go wrong by getting a hollow glass rod. They are light and cast as well as any other material and better than most. They are also strong and require little care.

The length of the rod will depend mostly on your personal preference if you are an experienced angler. The beginner will find it easier to cast with a short rod until he has mastered the technique. He will usually do best with a rod going 4½ or 5 ft. in length. At one time the short rods were all stiff in these lengths, and you had to get a long rod to get a light or limber action. Now you can get short rods with flexible actions. Most expert bait-casters prefer the longer rods going about 6 ft. in length. The majority of anglers settle for bait-casting rods running 5 or 5½ ft. in length.

Most manufacturers today label their bait-casting rods according to the action they have, showing whether they are light, medium, or heavy. There are variations among manufacturers, of course; and one firm's medium may be closer to heavy or the other way around. A much safer guide is to find out the range of lure weights a particular rod will cast. For the beginner or one-rod angler, the best bet is a medium action rod which will handle weights from about ½ oz. up to ¾ or even an oz. Such rods are available today in so-called "fast tapers" with a flexible tip tapering into a progressively more powerful mid-section and butt. The tip handles the lighter weight range of lures while more and more of the rod is brought into play as the lures get heavier.

Most bait-casting rods have cork-covered handles, and these are best for fishing. Some rods have metal or plastic handles, but these are cold to the touch and slippery when wet. The handles come in the straight and offset styles. A few old-timers and expert anglers prefer the straight rod handles. In these the reel seat is in a straight line with the handle. A bait-casting reel mounted on a straight handle is high, and you need big hands and long fingers to thumb and hold the rod with comfort. For most people the offset handle, which has the reel seat set below the level of the handle, is more comfortable. It also makes thumbing and casting easier and less tiring on the wrist.

A quick check of a bait-casting rod will include the guides to make sure they are properly aligned and not loose. You should also make certain that the reel you will use fits into the reel seat and locks securely in place.

Bait-casting rods are usually made in two pieces, either with a ferrule in the middle or a one-piece tip section and short handle. They are equally good except that the rod which separates in the middle is a bit easier to transport because of its shorter length. Before buying, make sure that the ferrules fit properly. They shouldn't be too loose or too tight.

The bait-casting reel is the most important item in the whole outfit. A well-made, smooth working reel allows you to get distance and accuracy into your casting; and it will last for years. There are many good models on the market from which you can choose.

The first bait-casting reels had no level-wind mechanism and posed a big problem in winding the line evenly on the spool during the retrieve. Anglers had to use the thumb and index finger of the left hand to do this and only a few became experts at this. If the line isn't wound on the spool evenly, the next cast usually causes a backlash and lands short. To solve this problem, reel makers added a level-winding device which guides the line back and forth across the spool and lays the line evenly on it. Today most bait-casting reels are equipped with such level-winding mechanisms.

When you buy a bait-casting reel, make sure that the level-wind works smoothly. It should also be protected by a cover to help keep out sand and grit. The level-wind mechanisms wear and often cause trouble. The pawl, which fits into the slots of the worm gear, should be easy to remove and replace with a new one. Some manufacturers supply a spare pawl to be carried with the reel.

At one time all bait-casting reels were made with heavy metal spools. The reason advanced was that such heavy spools turned longer and thereby gave more distance in casting. However, this proved wrong; and today most bait-casting reels are made with light spools of aluminum alloy or plastic and mounted on friction free bearings. Light spools start turning more quickly and easily and stop sooner. This results in fewer backlashes than when the heavy spools were used. And you can cast lighter lures with the lightweight spools since heavy spools require more weight and power to get under way. So when you choose a bait-casting reel, make sure that the spool starts easily when you flip the handle but also stops quickly. A heavy spool which turns for a long time when you flip the handle should be avoided.

Many bait-casting reels also have anti-backlash devices of various types. This is a braking device which automatically slows the reel spool so that it doesn't overrun and cause a backlash or bird's nest, or snarled line. On the better reels this anti-backlash device can be adjusted to match the weight of the lure being cast. Most such anti-backlash devices tend to slow down the start of the spool and its speed during the cast and often cut down the distance. So some expert anglers prefer reels without anti-backlash devices; or if they have one, they turn it off so that the spool runs freely without any hindrance. Despite some loss in distance, however, most beginners are much better off with a reel equipped with an anti-backlash device.

Some of the larger and more expensive bait-casting reels are equipped with drags or stars, which permit the fish to take line from the spool only under tension. Such reels are a great help in fighting a fish, especially a big or fast one. The drag can be adjusted by turning the star forward or backward.

Another feature found on a few reels is the free-spool lever which, when thrown off, allows only the spool to turn while the handle remains stationary.

When you buy a good bait-casting reel, you'll find that the gears and bearings are usually well made and of durable materials. Most modern reels are made of metals, plastics, or with corrosion-proof finishes which stand up well in fresh water. However, for salt water use you must be extra careful to get reels which will not corrode too readily. Even on the best reels some parts must be made from hard metal such as steel, and these parts should be easy to reach with oil or grease. Bait-casting reels vary in the ease of takedown for cleaning or oiling, and this should be checked before you buy the reel.

Some bait-casting reels hold up to 100 yd. of 12 or 14 lb. test braided line. If you plan to fish for big fish or in salt water, the entire spool can be filled with line. But if you use it mostly for black bass, trout, and panfish, you can buy only 50 yd. of line if you want. The space underneath the line can be filled with a "backing" of cheaper line or with a cork, balsa, or plastic arbor which fits over the reel spool spindle. Some bait-casting reels come equipped with this arbor, but if not you can buy one in almost any tackle store.

When buying a bait-casting outfit, you can skimp a bit on the rod and still get a good one for the job. But it's a smart idea to pay as much as you can afford to get a quality reel. For around $15.00 you'll get a serviceable reel, and if you spend $30.00 or $35.00 you'll have a top-notch product. Bait-casting reels run up to $50.00 in price for those equipped with special features and made of the best materials.

The motions of bait-casting are easy to follow, but good casting will take time. Simply hold the rod so that the reel handle faces up and your thumb rests on the reel spool. Lower the rod in front of you at about the 10 o'clock position, lining up the target with the rod tip. Then bring the rod back and up by raising the hand almost to the eye level by bending at the el-

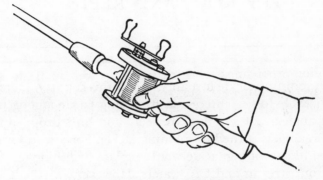

Holding bait-casting rod and reel

bow. When the rod reaches the vertical position, it should be stopped. As the weight of the lure bends the rod tip back, start the forward cast. As the rod tip drops, ease off with the thumb to release the lure. Then as the line moves out, keep a light pressure on the spool with your thumb. Finally, stop the rod at the 10 o'clock position; and when the lure hits the water, your thumb stops the spool.

The motions are easy, but the thumbing of the reel spool or line is the difficult part of bait-casting. A good caster "educates" his thumb so that it keeps the reel spool moving at the right speed at all times. Too much pressure will slow down the cast or stop it too soon. Too little will cause the spool to overrun and may result in a backlash. It requires a lot of practice to reach the stage where this thumbing becomes almost automatic. But once you achieve it, you fall into a class which few fresh-water anglers ever attain.

5

FLY RODS AND REELS

When spinning tackle first appeared in this country, there was a noticeable loss of interest in fly fishing tackle among fresh-water anglers. Sales of fly rods, reels, and lines dropped for a time as anglers turned to spinning tackle. For a while it even looked like spinning tackle would replace fly fishing tackle on our trout streams and bass waters. However, in recent years there has been a growing interest in fly fishing again; and many fresh-water anglers are buying fly rods, reels, and lines.

Most veteran fly fishermen, of course, never believed that spinning tackle would replace fly fishing tackle. They knew that when it comes to casting an artificial fly deliberately for trout you can't beat fly fishing tackle. Fly fishing is still the best method of catching trout when they are actively feeding on insects. The fly rod is also deadly for black bass when used with flies and bass bugs. And it is the type of rod allowed on most of the streams fished for Atlantic salmon. When it comes to real fun with such lightweights as panfish, you can't equal the sport provided by the long, flexible fly rod.

Fly rods have been made from a wide variety of materials in the past such as greenheart, lancewood, bethabara, lemon wood, ash, and other woods. Metals such as steel and various alloys were also tried but found unsuitable. When the first split-bamboo rods were made a century ago in this country, they became popular with fly casters and retained their popularity until after World War II.

Then, in 1946, Dr. Arthur M. Howald introduced the first fiber-glass rod; and the wonderful glass rods took over the market. The glass rods drove the cheap bamboo fly rods off the market. Then good Tonkin cane, which comes from Red China, became scarce; and even expert anglers who formerly used only split-bamboo rods turned to the better grade glass fly rods. Today there is still a handful of expert anglers who insist that nothing can duplicate the feel, action, and casting performance of a fine split-bamboo rod. In recent years, however, glass rods have been perfected until the difference in performance between split-bamboo and the better glass rods is so slight that it really doesn't matter too much. But there is a big difference in price—good split-bamboo fly rods cost more than the best glass fly rods.

A few companies still manufacture split-bamboo fly rods, usually on order. Such rods require the finest bamboo canes, selection of cane with thick walls, sawing, sanding, milling, gluing, and assembling. In fact, there are around fifty operations in the making of a first-class bamboo rod. Since many of these operations require handwork, it is easily seen why a fine split-bamboo rod costs so much. Split-bamboo fly rods of the best type today are a much finer product than those of say, twenty or thirty years ago. New designs and tapers and special waterproof glues and Bakelite impregnations make them more waterproof, decay-resistant, and stronger. Such rods, with proper care and barring accidents, will last a lifetime.

The average angler is not inclined to spend the money required to acquire a first-class split-bamboo rod. Nor does the average angler have the time, skill, or patience to give a good split-bamboo the proper care and handling it requires. Even many so-called "expert" anglers are hard on tackle and too hurried to "baby" a fine split-bamboo rod properly, so for most of these fishermen a glass fly rod is the most economical and practical.

Glass fly rods are not all alike in construction and vary according to the manufacturer. They differ in taper, wall-thickness, type of bonding agent, and proportion of glass to bonding agent. The cheaper hollow glass rods make use of thicker walls, and the glass cloth on such rods consists of coarser filaments. The result is a heavier rod with less glass and more resin. The better glass fly rods are made from a special glass cloth which consists of finer filaments, and the wall of the blank is thinner. This results in a lighter rod with more glass and less resin or bonding agent. A cheap glass fly rod may actually be stronger and even stand more abuse than an expensive rod. But it will rarely equal the "feel" and action of a top-grade glass fly rod. And the cheaper rods usually weigh more than the better glass fly rods of the same length.

The weight of a fly rod is an important matter, especially for the angler who fishes mostly with a dry fly, where continual false casting is required. Here the difference of an ounce or so can make a big difference at the end of the day. When fishing with wet flies or streamers or bass bugs, the weight factor isn't as crucial; but even here the trend is toward lighter rods.

The lightest and shortest fly rods usually range from 5½ to 7½ ft. in overall length and weigh from 1¾ to 4 oz. depending on the materials, length, and fittings used. Such rods are ideal for fishing small streams and ponds for small fish. They are best for small trout, panfish, and for use with the tiniest flies. A few expert anglers also use such light fly rods for large trout, bass, and salmon.

The medium range of fly rods runs from 7½ to 8½ ft. in length and weighs from 4 to 5½ oz. Rods in this class make up the bulk of the fly rods used for general trout fishing on streams and lakes. They are the nearest thing to an all-around fly rod which can be used for panfish, trout, and bass; for casting dry flies, wet flies, and streamers; and also for bass bags, baits, and other fly rod lures in a pinch.

The heavy fly rods run from 8½ to 9½ ft. in length and weigh anywhere from 5 to 7 oz. These are the "heavy-duty" power fly rods for fishing big waters where long casts are required and big fish are the rule. They are also used to cast heavy, bulky lures such as big wet flies, streamers or bucktails, and bass bugs. In this class you'll find the so-called "bass bug," "steelhead," and "salmon" fly rods. Many of these heavy fly rods can also be used for salt-water fishing.

There are also the special extra-long, heavy salmon fly rods ranging from 9 to 10½ ft. and weighing from 6 to 9 oz. which are made for one-handed casting. The heaviest fly rods made are the big, long, two-handed models designed for big waters and large salmon. These range anywhere from 11 to 16 ft. and weigh from 10 to 20 oz. However, these rods are waning in popularity; and very few manufacturers make them nowadays in this country. They are still widely used on European waters where long casts, big fish, and heavy flies make the two-handed salmon rods a necessity. But for most Canadian and Maine salmon streams, the shorter, lighter, one-handed salmon rods from 8½ to 9½ ft. will handle most fishing situations.

Abercrombie & Fitch also sells what it calls a "Banty" fly rod which is only 4 ft., 4 in. and weighs 1 oz. It is designed for small stream fishing and for casting in tight places where there is little room for the longer fly rods.

Fly rods are made in various types of actions; and these have been called "dry-fly," "wet-fly," and "bass" actions. Or you will hear the expressions "fast action" and "slow action" used. At one time the wet fly or slow action fly rods were common. These were the soft, willowy types which were used for fishing with wet flies. Such rods bent into a wide circle right down to the butt or handle.

The dry fly or fast action fly rod is stiffer, and most of the bend is in the tip section. Such rods are best when false casting is required to dry the fly.

Choosing the best action fly rod for any particular person is difficult because you have to consider personal preferences, the type of fishing being done, casting habits, and other factors. So while one angler will prefer a dry-fly action fly rod for all his fishing, another may lean toward a wet-fly action fly rod.

The tendency nowadays is toward a dry-fly action fly rod for most trout fishing, whether using dry flies, wet flies, nymphs, or streamers. Most rod manufacturers make this dry fly type of fly rod. Actually, some of these rods, although labeled "dry fly" rods, may be more of an in-between action. They are not as fast as a true dry-fly action rod or as slow as a true wet-fly action rod. They often work well for both dry and wet-fly fishing as well as for other fly rod lures.

Fly rods used for black bass, steelhead, and salmon should have the power to cast heavier lines and bulkier lures for good distances even against a strong wind. Most of this fishing is done with wet flies, streamers, or bass bugs. Here a rod with a slow action is best to cast such lures most efficiently.

The length of the fly rod you choose will also depend on personal preferences and the type of casting and fishing you do. As a general rule, the shorter, lighter rods are best for small streams, narrow spaces, short casts, and for dry-fly fishing. The longer, more powerful rods are best for big streams, rivers, and lakes and anywhere else where long casts and a long line must be handled. The longer rods not only make casting easier by keeping the backcast high but also enable the angler to handle and manipulate the lures better on a longer line. So they are best suited for fishing wet flies, streamers, and bass bugs.

However, not everyone can handle the longer, heavier rods without tiring the wrist or arm. So for many persons the lighter, shorter fly rods are best. Luckily, nowadays with the newer modern glass rods you can find fly rods in the 7½, 8, and 8½ ft.

lengths to handle almost every kind of fishing. Most beginners buying their first fly rod can safely get an 8-ft. rod to start with. This can be used for trout, bass, panfish, and even for steelhead and salmon occasionally. Later on, if the angler desires a shorter or longer fly rod, he can add to his collection. But an 8-ft. fly rod is the nearest thing to an all-around length for most fly fishing.

The fittings on a fly rod should be examined carefully before purchase. The number of guides on a fly rod will vary, depending on its length, action, and quality. The usual number will vary from five to sixteen, with fewer guides found on the cheaper rods than on the more expensive ones. Most fly rods will have anywhere from eight to twelve guides. Whatever the number, there should be enough guides to hold the line close to the curvature of the rod along its entire length. The guides should be of hard metal and should be large enough to permit the fly line to move freely through them. Stainless steel guides are best for both fresh and salt water use.

There are many designs of the cork grips and handles used on fly rods. One of the most common types is the "cigar"-shaped cork handle, which is thickest in the middle and tapers on both ends. Other types of handles are shaped to accommodate the thumb or palm of the hand. Most fly rod handles are round, but others are oval-shaped. The type you choose will depend on your own personal preference. It should feel comfortable when gripped in your hand. Nearly all fly rod handles are made from cork, which should be of top grade quality.

The reel seat on a fly rod should be made from lightweight metal or plastic, and it should hold the reel firmly in place. The locking reel seats are best, but make sure that they fit the fly reel you have.

The ferrules on a fly rod should be made of lightweight metal, and they should fit snugly. Ferrules that are too loose or too tight will cause trouble later on. Fly rods come in two or three sections, and the one you choose isn't too important. The three-piece rods break into shorter sections for easier transporting. Some special fly rods are even made in four sections for the traveling angler. The two-piece fly rod is a bit lighter and may have slightly better action, but these differences mean little to the average angler.

An important item often neglected when buying a fly rod is the case. Even the best and strongest fly rod is fragile and delicate. It deserves protection when being transported, stored, or when not in use. A tough fiber, plastic, or light metal case should be purchased separately if the rod doesn't come with one originally.

When it comes to buying a fly rod, it's wise to spend as much as you can afford for a top product. Although a serviceable glass fly rod can be bought for around $20.00, it's better to spend twice as much. Such a rod will usually be a bit lighter, have better action, and will be made from parts which not only look better but last longer.

Fly reels are made in two types—single action and automatic. The single-action fly reel makes one revolution of the spool for each turn of the handle. To cast with this reel, you strip line by hand from the spool and then wind it back by hand. Such reels are simply made, durable, and have deep, narrow spools holding plenty of line. The spool revolves on a shaft; and the reel usually has a click, line guard, one or two handles, and a foot plate to fit the reel seat. Most of the larger and more expensive fly reels also have an adjustable drag for applying tension on the line. This drag should be smooth and dependable if used for big fish. Fly reels will vary in size and weight, running from 3 oz. for the smaller types up to 10 oz. or more for the larger ones. Spool widths will vary in diameter from $2\frac{7}{8}$ in. up to 4 in. Naturally, for use with a light fly rod and dry fly fishing where plenty of casting is required, the lightest and smallest fly reels will be best. But for heavier fishing such as bass, steelhead, big trout, and salmon, the larger reels are required. Line capacity is important if you fish for fast running and long running fish such as steelhead and salmon. For catching small or medium-sized trout and bass, you can get away with about 100 yd. of backing under your regular fly line. But for big trout, steelhead, and salmon, you need a reel holding at least 150 or 200 yd. of backing line.

Many of the better single action fly reels have interchangeable spools. Here you can buy an extra spool or two and change fly lines at will. One spool can have a floating double-tapered line, another a sinking line, and a third a weight-forward line. The extra spools can be carried in your pocket until needed for a particular kind of fishing situation.

The automatic type fly reels operate with springs which retrieve the line after it has been stripped off the reel. You still use your hand to strip line from the reel; but instead of winding it back by hand, it is automatically wound back by merely pressing a trigger or lever. Most of the automatics have a free-stripping device which enables you to pull the line off the reel even though the spring is fully wound.

Which fly reel is best—the single action or the automatic? For ordinary fishing for small trout or panfish, it really doesn't make much difference which type you choose. Actually, when fishing from a boat or shore for small trout, bass, or panfish, the automatic fly reel is more convenient and prevents line tangles when loose coils are draped all over the boat or grass.

But when it comes to fly fishing for big fish in fast currents where long runs are expected, the single-action reel is best. It holds more line and enables the angler to maintain a constant tension on a fish. Automatic fly reels have a limited spring retrieve for short distances. If a big fish takes too much line off such a reel, you won't be able to get it all back on. So for ordinary small trout fishing or bass bug fishing, get either a single-action or an automatic fly reel. For big trout, steelhead, or salmon, get a large single-action fly reel.

For small fish a cheap fly reel will serve as well as an expensive one since it simply acts as a line holder, and you don't have to use it to play the fish. When going after the big fish, however, a better made, more expensive fly reel will perform more smoothly and prove more dependable.

The best single action fly reels are made in England, and you can spend anywhere from $10.00 to $100 for such a reel. Several good single action fly reels are also made in this country. And, of course, if you buy an automatic fly reel, you'll find the widest assortment and some fine ones made in the United States.

After you get a good fly rod and reel, you need a fly line. These are covered in detail in Chapter 7.

When you have your complete fly fishing outfit, it's not of much use unless you learn how to use it. This means being able to cast a fly a good distance with finesse and delicacy. Fly casting is not difficult if you start off right in the beginning. If you get instructions from an expert or friend who knows how to cast, that is the best way to learn. But if you have no one to teach you, it is possible to learn in time from written instructions and diagrams.

Fly casters hold the rod in two different ways. One method is to grasp the cork grip on the rod with the right hand and let the thumb rest on top. The other method is to grasp the cork grip with the thumb on the side. Either method is satisfactory —try both and choose the one you prefer.

To cast, assemble your rod and string the fly line through the guides. In the beginning it is not necessary to add a fly leader to the end of the line, but later on it will help. You can practice casting on a lawn at first since you can handle the line better in front of you. The first step is to strip some line off your reel and pull it out at the tip of the rod. About 20 or 25 feet will be

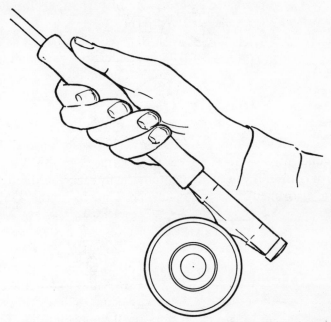

Most common grip used on fly rod. Some casters also hold thumb on side

enough to start. Then carry this line out in front of you and
pull it so that it lies straight on the ground. Now point the rod
at the target in front of you. Then, with a sharp upward and
backward motion with your wrist and forearm, pick the line
off the ground and let it fly above and behind you. Try to see
if you can make the line sail straight up into the air over your
head. It won't do this; but by trying, you'll get a high back cast,
which is important. As the line moves back, stop your rod
when it reaches a point directly over your head (12 o'clock).
The rod will drift behind you; but when learning how to cast,
don't let it go too far back.

As the line starts unrolling behind you and when it is almost
straight (you'll feel a pull on the rod tip), start the forward cast
by pushing the rod ahead with your wrist and arm. In the be-

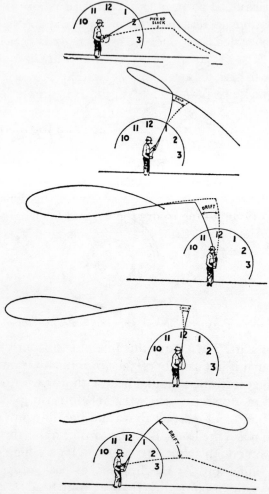

The steps in fly casting, shown from top to bottom

ginning it's a good idea to turn around and watch the line to see if it's almost straight before you begin the forward cast. As the line sails ahead of you, follow through with the rod.

This is the basic overhead cast, and you can easily master it with practice until you can cast 30 ft. of line out. There are many variations such as the roll cast, side cast, and steeple cast, which can be tried later, once the fundamental overhead cast is mastered. A good way to get the feel and timing of the fly line in the air is to practice false casts. This is done by casting exactly the same way as in the overhead cast. But instead of letting the line touch the ground, you let it come within a foot or two of the grass and then immediately lift it up for the back cast again. You can wave the rod forward and backward for several minutes without touching the ground or water in front of you or behind you. When you can do this smoothly, you have acquired the feel needed for ordinary fly casting. False casting is used in dry fly fishing to dry the fly, and for lengthening or shortening the line so that the lure can be placed exactly where wanted.

6

OTHER FRESH-WATER TACKLE

Although most of the emphasis in the fishing tackle field is on fancy rods, reels, lines, and lures, millions of fresh water anglers still use simple poles when fishing. The ordinary fishing pole with a length of line tied to the end and a hook attached to the line has been used for centuries. Basically such outfits have changed little through the years, but several innovations and improvements have been made in recent years.

The simplest fishing pole is a long, one-piece bamboo stick running anywhere from 8 to 20 ft. in length. Such cane poles are still popular with country kids and local fishermen who live near a stream, river, or lake and have no transportation problems. For those who must travel any distance, however, such long, one-piece cane poles are cumbersome and present difficulties.

For such anglers the sectional or sliding poles, available in various lengths, are the answer. Some merely have graduated sections which fit into each other. Others have metal ferrules which fit together to make a long rod but can be broken down into three or four sections for easy carrying. Still others have screw threads which join the sections together. Most of these poles are made from bamboo and are imported from Japan or other Eastern countries. Some of them are equipped with guides and reel seats for mounting a reel, but most are lacking in these. However, it is a simple matter to wind on or strap on guides or reel seat with thread or tape. You can also use reel clamps to hold a reel in place on a cane pole.

In recent years many fishing tackle companies have come out with telescopic glass poles. These usually collapse to a short length anywhere from 3 to 5 ft. for carrying but extend to lengths from 10 to 20 ft. There are usually anywhere from two to five sections which slide into each other or connect. Some of these also come with line guides, reel seats, or line winders; but other types lack these and are plain.

Cane or glass poles are used mostly for still fishing with live bait; but they can also be used for skittering with pork rind, pork chunk, spoons, or spinners. The longer, heavier lengths are best when fishing from shore or a pier where the pole can be propped up when not in use. But when fishing from a boat, the shorter, lighter poles are easier and less tiring to use.

Fresh-water pole fishermen also use many types of floats or bobbers for their fishing. The cork ball or pear-shaped cork floats are old-time favorites and are still available in various sizes. Some of these are plain, while others are painted, usually red and white. The plain round cork floats usually have a peg in a hole to keep the cork in place on the line. The pear or egg-shaped floats have a longer stick or rod running through the hole.

There are also many plastic imitations of these cork floats and bobbers on the market. These usually have some kind of slot or clip on the ends to attach to the line and can be adjusted to move up and down whenever needed.

In recent years many round plastic floats have appeared on the market. These are strong, durable, and simple to attach to the line. Many of them have plungers or push-buttons which, when worked, permit a small wire hook to emerge for attaching to the line. These come in various diameters and sizes from $5/8$ to $2\frac{1}{4}$ in. for all kinds of fresh-water fishing.

The old-time porcupine quill floats are still used for light tackle fishing, especially for minnows or for wary fish. The natural quills still haven't been surpassed in lightness and thinness, but many balsa wood or plastic imitations have been introduced for the still fishing enthusiasts.

Finally, we have the various plastic bubble floats, which are transparent and either round or oval. Some of these have little plugs which can be removed so that the float can be filled with water to provide weight for casting. Others have spring-loaded plungers that are pushed in to permit the water to enter. These floats are popular not only with still fishermen but also with spinning anglers, who cast baits or small flies or panfish bugs with them. They can be used empty or filled to provide the proper amount of weight for the bait or lure you are using.

Other special fresh-water fishing rods include the various telescopic spinning, bait-casting, and fly rods. The steel telescopic rods were quite popular many years ago but have now disappeared from the scene. They have been replaced by glass telescopic rods. While such rods are very convenient to store, transport and use, they have disadvantages. Because of the step-down in diameter between sections, the action of telescopic rods is not as good as that found on regular rods which have a smooth gradual taper. And most telescopic rods do not have enough line guides for proper casting and fighting of fish. These drawbacks are not too serious in the case of spinning or bait-casting rods but show up most in telescopic fly rods.

Still other special types of rods are used for fresh-water trolling. Here, though, the great majority of anglers make use of their regular fishing tackle. Fly rods, for example, are used to troll baits and streamers and bucktail flies for land-locked salmon, trout, and bass. Spinning and bait-casting rods are used in trolling for a wide variety of fresh-water species. Although many of these rods will serve the purpose, as a rule they are too limber to make good trolling rods. A rod is subjected to more

Many fishing tackle manufacturers put up fishing kits which contain the rod, reel, line, lures, and instructions needed to start fishing. These are very popular with beginners and gift buyers.

Sweetheart tubular glass spinning rod by Wright & McGill comes in two pieces and in 6½ and 7 ft. lengths.

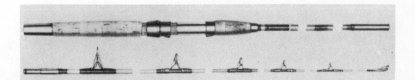

Heddon Sturdy tubular glass spinning rod is made for heavier fresh-water fishing. It comes in two pieces and is 6 ft. 9 in. long. It has a fixed reel seat and long tapered rear grip of specie cork.

1. Grab line with the index finger of the right hand and push the bail on the reel down with your left hand.

2. Point rod tip at the target and get set to cast.

3. Bring the rod up quickly and sharply, using mostly wrist action.

4. Stop the rod at approximately the 1 o'clock position as shown.

5. Now bring the rod down with a snap toward the original position in front of you, releasing the line from your finger.

6. Stop the cast by putting your index finger on the spool, and start the retrieve with your left hand.

South Bend Norseman spin-casting reel is a heavy duty fresh-
water and salt-water model which
handles monofilament lines up
to 20 lb. Pfleuger "88" enclosed
spinning reel has precision machined stainless steel gears and
features immediate line control.
South Bend Futura spin-cast reel
features twin triggers for casting
with either hand. It also has a
reversible crank and can be
changed for use as a conventional
spinning reel.

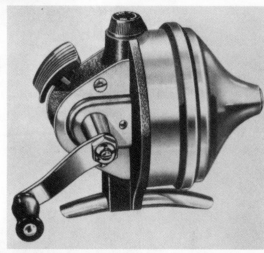

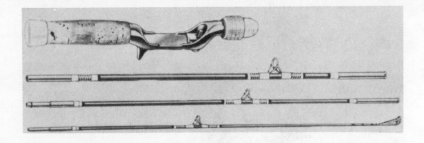

True Temper Flipline Traveler solid glass spin-casting rod breaks down into four sections, each 16 in. long. Assembled, it is 4½ ft. long.

South Bend Powerflex spin cast rod is 7 ft. long and comes in three sections. The butt section is made from a light metal alloy, and the rest of the rod is hollow glass.

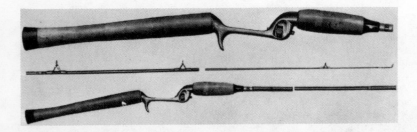

Wright & McGill Deep Water special duty spin-casting rod comes in 6 and 8 ft. lengths and is designed for casting and trolling. It has an extra long 10 in. cork butt grip.

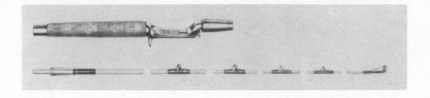

Heddon Musky Special tubular casting rod is a 5-ft. heavy duty rod with one-piece tip. It has an 8 in. rear grip designed for casting heavier lures and fighting big fish.

Left. Pfleuger Supreme bait-casting reel is an old favorite, with over a million reels already manufactured and sold. It features gears and bearings made of phosphor bronze, jeweled oil cups, and lightweight cast aluminum spool.

Right. Langley Lurecast bait-casting reel is a narrow spool, lightweight, level-wind reel designed for light lines and lures.

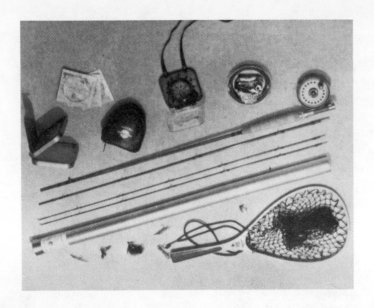

Orvis Battenkill fly rods are made from split bamboo impregnated with bakelite resin to make them waterproof. They are available in all lengths and actions from 7 to 9½ ft.

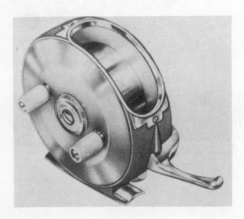

Ocean City automatic fly reel by True Temper can be converted to single-action by turning a knob.

Pfleuger Medalist is a long-time favorite fly reel of the single-action type. It has an aluminum frame, drag, and interchangeable spool.

strain when trolling than when just casting. This is especially true when trolling with long lines, wire lines, or weights and sinkers. Also, when trolling deep, you often get hung up on the bottom; and the sudden shock may break a rod with a thin, limber tip. The same thing can happen when a big fish hits the lure.

You can still use the bait-casting and spinning rods for trolling in fresh water; but instead of using the lightest models, get those that are heavier. The heavy-duty fresh-water bait-casting and spinning rods can be used for many kinds of trolling. This is especially true when you use a small, light lure for shallow trolling.

For big lures, big fish, and for deeper trolling with weights, you can get the special trolling rods. These are similar to bait-casting rods except that they have a straight instead of an offset reel seat and a longer handle or butt and a foregrip. The rod can be anywhere from 5 to 7 ft. long and should be fairly stiff.

Similar rods are used to catch pike and muskies in many lakes and rivers. These two fish have tough jaws, and it takes a pretty stiff rod to set the big hooks used on lures for these fish. So here again the heavier type bait-casting rods, spinning rods, and special musky rods are best for this fishing. Many of the so-called "popping" rods used in salt-water fishing in the Gulf of Mexico and Florida can be used for big pike and muskies. They make good all-around heavy-duty rods for casting or trolling.

For deep trolling such as for lake trout in 100 to 500 ft. of water, you may need a still heavier rod. Many anglers resort to the lighter salt-water trolling pier or boat rods. Trolling at such depths requires the use of weights or wire lines; and light, limber, fresh-water rods are not suitable for such work.

When it comes to reels used for trolling, here again many regular fly, spinning, and bait-casting reels can be used for light trolling near the surface. But when you go deeper, the larger heavy-duty bait-casting reels and salt-water reels are better. A star-drag and free-spool are handy to have when trolling deep; and although a few fresh-water reels are equipped with such devices, they are more commonly found on salt-water reels. Some of the larger level-wind reels are also suitable for fresh-water trolling. When using wire lines for deep trolling, the salt-water reels holding at least 200 to 300 yd. of 36-lb. test lines are best. They should have a metal spool, which is stronger than a plastic type.

There are also special single-action, narrow spool reels made for fresh-water trolling. They hold up to 500 yd. of wire line and retrieve the line rapidly from deep water. The narrow spools on such reels also keep the line from slipping and snarling too readily. Such reels are used primarily when trolling deep for such fish as lake trout.

Fresh-water anglers also resort to the use of hand lines, trot lines, and so-called drop lines, mostly for bottom fishing for catfish, carp, buffalo, sturgeon, and similar heavy fish. They also use various types of salt-water fishing outfits for big fish which may prove too much for the lighter fresh-water outfits. For such fishing you can choose from some of the salt-water fishing tackle covered in second half of this book.

7

FRESH-WATER LINES

The progress and development made in such fishing tackle as rods, reels, and lures is evident; and most anglers are aware of it. But the improvements made in fishing lines are not so noticeable on the surface, and only when you compare the older lines with the newer ones do you get a true picture of the progress made in recent years.

The earlier fresh-water lines were made from hair, silk, linen, cotton, and other plant and animal fibers. Some of these materials are still being used to make fishing lines. However, the development of synthetic and chemical substances such as nylon and dacron has given us fishing lines far superior to the older types.

The advance in fishing lines is evident when we consider the latest fly lines. The earlier fly lines were made with silk cores and were oil-impregnated. They were heavy, many of the finishes used peeled or cracked, and the silk core was subject to deterioration with age or when used in salt water.

The earlier fly lines made for dry-fly fishing were also difficult to keep afloat. They required constant dressing to keep them floating even for a short time.

Modern fly lines are made with nylon or dacron cores, do not rot or deteriorate with age, and can be used in salt water as well as fresh. They are lighter and softer than the earlier silk fly lines. The result is a fly line which is a pleasure to cast and which floats for long periods.

Modern fly lines are now made either to float or to sink. The floating lines are usually made with nylon cores, which are sealed with surface coatings to create watertight compartments or centers. The cores are either hollow or have tiny bubbles which provide the buoyancy to keep the line afloat. The floating lines are best for fishing with dry flies or bass bugs.

The sinking type fly lines have cores of silk, dacron, or spun glass. This gives them greater weight, and the absence of hollow spaces makes them sink fast. Sinking fly lines are used for wet flies, nymphs, streamers, bucktails, live bait, and other fly lures which are to be fished deep.

Three kinds of tapers are found on most fly lines: level, double-taper, and weight-forward. The weight-forward fly tapers are also called torpedo head, three-diameter, tadpole, and bug tapers.

The level lines are of the same diameter throughout the entire length of line. Years ago they were popular for fishing with live bait and for casting bass bugs and heavy fly rod lures such as spoons, spinners, and streamers. Some anglers still use level lines for such fishing; but they do not shoot as well as tapered lines when distance is required, and they also land with a splash. Since they are the cheapest of fly lines, they often serve as a beginner's line until he learns how to cast well enough to use a tapered line.

The double-tapered fly line tapers to a thin line on both ends and is heavy in the middle section. The heavy middle section or belly provides casting weight, while the thin tapered end lands on the water lightly and delicately with the least disturbance. A double-tapered line is also easier to pick off the water. When one end becomes worn, you can reverse the line and use the other end. Double-tapered fly lines are a must for dry fly fishing but are also versatile and can be used for shallow nymph or wet-fly fishing, streamers, bucktails, and other fly rod lures.

The weight-forward or torpedo head line is a three-diameter taper which has a short thin taper on the extreme end, a heavier belly for casting weight, and then a long, thin, level section which is the shooting line. Weight-forward lines come in many different proportions depending on the manufacturer. However, they can be broken down into two main divisions: those which have long tapers and bellies in front of the shooting or running lines and those which have short tapers and bellies in front. The long tapers and bellies are best for fishing with small flies, while those with short tapers and bellies are used for bass bugs and other big fly lures which offer wind resistance. Both lines are made for distance casting and will reach out farther than level or double-tapered lines.

Fly line sizes have been designated in the past by the use of the alphabet letters A, B, C, D, E, F, G, H, and I. The A line is the thickest while the I line is the thinnest in diameter. This method was fairly reliable when all fly lines were made with silk cores and oil-impregnated coatings. The C line made by one manufacturer was almost the same in diameter and weight as the C line made by other fishing line companies. But with the advent of nylon and dacron as fly line materials and of various plastic coatings, this reliability has changed; and there are often great variations in the diameters and weights of the various fly lines made by different manufacturers.

There is a growing movement to do away with the alphabet numbering system for fly lines and substitute one which would indicate the weight of a given length of fly line instead. However, until this is done, most manufacturers are continuing the use of alphabet letters to indicate the size of the fly line.

Thus a level fly line will usually be some letter from B to G. A double-tapered line will be an HEH, HDH, HCH, GBG, or

GAG, while a three-diameter line will be HEG, HDG, HCF, GBF, or GAF.

In fly fishing, of course, it's the weight of the fly line itself which is cast; and the lure weight or bulk actually retards the cast instead of helping it. So it is important to get the correct fly line size for the fly rod you are using. The best way to do this is to try different fly lines until you locate the best one for your particular rod. Some tackle dealers in the smaller towns keep the various sizes on reels to let you try casting with the line. In large cities this is often impossible; so you have to try to determine the correct size by other means.

In stores where the salesman is an experienced fly angler, you can usually depend on his advice. If the salesman is not informed, the next best thing is to follow the manufacturer's advice. Most fishing rod companies indicate the fly line size which will fit their fly rods. Those that make or sell fly lines are the most dependable in this respect. Many fly line manufacturers also put out literature or booklets which recommend specific fly lines for different length and action fly rods.

For bait-casting reels and for some kinds of spinning, there are different kinds of braided lines on the market. At one time the only line available for bait-casting reels was the silk braided line. The newer synthetic nylon and dacron lines have now almost replaced silk lines for this fishing. They are stronger, more waterproof, resist rot, and do not deteriorate with age. The earlier braided nylon lines had quite a bit of stretch and were somewhat stiff, but the newer ones have been greatly improved in this respect. They are also waterproofed and heat treated to obtain extra strength and a smaller diameter.

Braided nylon bait-casting lines come in various colors and strengths for almost any kind of fresh-water fishing. They can be bought in tests from 6 to 72 lb. The lighter tests from 6 to 18 lb. are most popular for casting, while the heavier tests are used for pike, muskies, and for trolling and still fishing. You can get them in almost any color, but black and gray lines are the most popular.

Some line companies also put out braided nylon and dacron lines for spinning reels. They are used by some anglers when fishing with weighted bass bugs, popping plugs, and similar surface lures where you reel with jerks, pauses, and even stop while the lure lies on top without moving. Under such conditions, braided lines tend to spool better on the reel than monofilament lines and cause less trouble. But the monofilament lines have been greatly improved and are much softer and limper than the earlier kinds. So the great majority of fresh-water anglers prefer to use the monofilament lines.

For all-around use the monofilament lines can't be beat. In this country most monofilament lines are made from Du Pont nylon, which is processed, labeled, and dyed by various line companies under different trade names. Each company claims his product is superior and gives the reasons why. Although basically made from the same raw material, they do vary somewhat in strength for a given diameter, stretch, smoothness, limpness, softness, hardness, etc., depending on what is done to the line.

There are also imported monofilament lines such as perlon, platyl and others which are sold in this country. The platyl monofilament line is very popular with fresh and salt-water anglers and comes in various strengths for this fishing. It is thin, limp, and strong with a minimum of stretch.

Dupont also makes a monofilament called "Stren" which has a smaller diameter than the orginal nylon monofilament and is also limper and has less stretch. It comes in tests from 2 to 30 lb. and is pale gunmetal gray in color, which is almost invisible in the water. It is made in a round shape and in the newer oval shape, which is supposed to lie better on conventional revolving spool reels and give less trouble in casting and spooling than the round type monofilaments.

Although monofilament lines are recommended mostly for spinning with open- and closed-type spinning reels, more and more bait-casters are also using them. The new extra limp or relaxed round and oval monofilament lines are best to use with revolving spool reels.

Then we have the weighted and wire lines which are used in fresh-water trolling in deep water. For shallow water trolling, fly lines, braided lines, and monofilament lines used for casting often work well. Often all that is needed is the weight of the lure and an added sinker or trolling weight. But if you really want to get down deep, you must use a weighted or wire line. One type of line which has been used for trolling is the lead core line. The center of the line is lead, while the outside consists of a woven sheath of nylon. The lead, of course, adds the weight but no strength, which is mainly in the nylon. Lead core lines are easier to handle than other types of wire lines and do not kink or spring off the reel under tension. However, they are not as good for very deep water as other types.

Wire lines have been made from different metals such as bronze, copper, stainless steel, and Monel. The Monel or nickel alloy wire lines are enjoying a great popularity today. You'll find wire lines mostly in braided, twisted, and solid kinds. The braided wire line is bulkier than the other two. It doesn't sink as deep as twisted or solid wire lines but is easier to handle on the reel.

The twisted wire lines, of course, consist of a number of strands of copper, stainless steel, or Monel twisted together like a cable. They are also thicker in diameter than solid lines and do not sink as fast or as deep as the solid line. But they are easier to use than solid wire and can be manhandled with less danger of kinking and breaking.

The solid wire lines have become very popular in recent years and are now used for many kinds of trolling. They are thin, strong, and sink fast and deep when trolled, even in a current.

Solid wire lines are usually made from stainless steel or Monel and come in tests from 5 to 100 lb. or more. They are much harder to handle on a reel than the other types of wire lines because they kink and jump off the reel spool.

The size or strength of casting or trolling lines you buy will depend on several factors: the weight of the lures you will cast, the weight and action of the rod, where the fishing will be done, how big and what kind of fish you will catch, and whether you are a novice or an expert angler.

For example, the ultra-light lines testing from ½ lb. to 4 lb. must be used with tackle to match. The rod must be flexible and light, the reel should be small and have a sensitive drag, and the lures should weigh only from $\frac{1}{32}$ to $\frac{1}{4}$ oz. Even with the proper tackle, it requires a lot of skill and experience to fish with such hairlines. So until an angler acquires this skill he should stick to heavier lines and tackle.

If you are an average fisherman using an open-faced reel, you'll do best with lines testing 4 to 6 lb. in monofilament. With closed-faced reels you can use 8 or 10 lb. test lines. However, when the waters are very weedy or when going after bigger fish such as pike, muskies, lake trout, or carp, you can change to an 8 or 10 lb. test line for the open-faced reels and to 12 or 15 lb. test lines for the closed-faced reels.

The weight of the lures and the action of the rod also determine line strength. The shock of casting heavy lures and setting the hook in a fish's mouth or playing a fish requires a heavier line than if a light, flexible rod and small lure are used. Just setting the big hooks used on pike or musky plugs or lures requires a stiffer rod and stronger line than for other fish.

In open waters where a fish is allowed to run freely, you can land lunkers on light lines. But in snag-infested waters with weeds, stumps, logs, rocks, etc., you need heavier lines to slow down or turn a fish away.

The size of the fish which are running also governs the size of the line. If the trout in a stream or bass in a lake are small or if fishing for panfish, you can use light lines. If the fish are big bass, pike, muskies, carp, or catfish, then you can use heavier lines.

In trolling you use heavier lines than when casting, first because in casting the lighter lines give you more distance, and second because trolling places a greater strain on a line. The fish is hooked when the boat is moving, and the sudden shock can snap a light line. Also, you often get hung up in sunken trees, logs, weeds, and rocks; and this also strains the line.

Finally, the skill of the angler also determines line strength. A beginner is better off with a slightly stronger line until he learns how to cast and to play a fish. An expert with a light outfit and line can often make "stunt" catches which a beginner shouldn't even attempt. It takes quite a bit of experience before you can judge just how much strain a light line will take before breaking. But even the experts lose some nice fish with light tackle because of broken lines. If you want the most sport and fun, you have to expect that.

8

FRESH-WATER LURES

Artificial lures have been used in fishing for food for thousands of years, and anglers have been using them in sport fishing for several hundred years. But it is mainly in the last century that artificial lures have become popular and mostly in the last fifty years that they have been manufactured commercially in large numbers. Now, however, they are sold in the millions, if not billions; and there are so many different kinds of fresh-water lures on the market that it is almost impossible to cover them all.

Today when an angler walks into a well-stocked fishing tackle store and examines the many lures on the counter, under the counter, and on the shelves, he scratches his head in bewilderment. He asks such questions as: Which lures should I buy? What shape, size, weight, color, or finish? What's best for this species or that? An attempt will be made to answer most of these questions in this chapter so that the average angler can make a wise selection for the fishing he plans to do.

Most lures are designed to look like something to eat from a fish's standpoint. They try to represent an insect, worm, crayfish, frog, minnow or small fish, mouse, or similar animal. Other lures, however, look like nothing on this earth; yet they often catch fish. Whether fish mistake them for food or strike for another reason is not definitely known. Observations and studies have shown that some fish may strike due to force of habit, curiosity, or anger. The fact remains that artificial lures in the hands of an expert angler who knows fish habits and lure manipulation will catch more and bigger fish than anglers depending on live or natural baits.

Many lures have their own "built-in" action. Others must be activated by the angler or the flow of water. Some are designed to work on the surface, others just under the surface, and still others down deep near the bottom. Each lure works best under certain conditions and with certain tackle and for specific fish. Often the angler will hit the right combination by luck. Experience will also teach an angler which lure is best under prevailing conditions and waters and for which fish.

Today the angler who fishes streams, rivers, ponds, or lakes carries a good assortment of lures to meet most fishing conditions. Tackle boxes have grown bigger and bigger to accommodate all these lures.

When it comes to the artificial flies, we have so many different patterns that have been tied over a period of several hundred years that it would take several volumes just to list and describe them. The perfect fly hasn't been tied yet and probably never will be. But that doesn't keep anglers from trying, and every amateur fly tier has a pet creation or two. Most fly patterns have a very short life. They are tied by the individual angler, catch some fish, then are recommended to friends, who copy them. They may even be tied commercially by professional fly tiers for a while. But in the great majority of cases, after enjoying a brief period of local popularity, they die out and are soon forgotten.

The flies which have survived the test of time proved their worth in many areas over a long period. Many originated in England long ago, while others are recent creations in this country. Most of them have specific uses under certain fishing conditions.

Flies can be divided into two main groups. The first includes the dry flies, which are fished on the surface of the water. The second consists of wet flies, which are fished below the surface.

Flies also fall into two other separate classes: the imitations and the attractors. The imitations represent natural insects or other fish foods as closely as possible. They are sparsely tied and drab in color since most natural insects are delicate and subtle in color. The imitations usually work best when fish are actually feeding on a particular food and you can match this in size, outline, and color.

The attractor flies are more bulky, gaudy in color, and actually represent no particular creature. These so-called "fancy" patterns often bring a rise from a fish which is not on the feed. Whether they are mistaken for something to eat or merely make a fish angry or curious is not known. But the fact remains that they produce often enough to make carrying them worthwhile.

Although they are called "flies," not all such lures are made to represent insects. Some of them imitate worms, tiny frogs, crayfish, tiny fish, or minnows more than they do the insects.

Dry flies are designed to float on top of the water. They are tied to represent various adult insects which are just leaving the water, hatching, laying their eggs, or have fallen on the water. Dry flies have long, stiff, glossy hackles and tails which support them on the water. They are also tied on light wire hooks and are daubed with fly dressing to help them stay afloat. A good dry fly will support itself on the hackle and tail when placed on a table. When dropped from a height, it will bounce on a flat surface.

There are different kinds or types of dry flies. The conventional dry fly is the divided wing, which has two erect, separate wings in an upright position, a collar of stiff hackle, a body, and a tail. This fly is supposed to represent the adult May fly.

It works best when these insects are actually hatching or laying eggs on the water.

Other types of dry flies include the fan wing, hairwing, hairbody, spent wing, variant, spider, bivisible, and the midge. There are variations in construction and materials used in tying these flies which result in differences making them suitable for specific kinds of fishing conditions. Some work best on quiet pools or smooth, glassy stretches. Others are best for working the rapids or other rough water spots.

When it comes to choosing certain patterns among the different types of flies, local preferences and conditions are usually taken into consideration. Any good tackle dealer in your area who stocks dry flies will tell you which ones work best there. Some of the dry flies which have stood the test of time and catch fish in scattered areas include the following: Quill Gordon, Adams, Light Cahill, Fanwing Royal Coachman, Hendrickson, Gray Wulff, Royal Wulff, Brown Spider, Red Variant, Black Bivisible, Brown Bivisible, Black Gnat, and Black Midge. That's a good basic dozen to start with, and you can catch fish in many parts of the country on these if you get them in different sizes. But if you're like most anglers, you'll soon add others. Dry flies in sizes 10, 12, 14, and 16 are most widely used; but some of the smaller flies may be tied on No. 18 or 20 hooks.

Dry flies are best during the late spring, summer, or early fall, when insect life is abundant and natural flies are found in abundance. The fastest action takes place when trout are rising and feeding on hatching flies and you can imitate the fly they are taking. However, some good fishing often takes place when trout are not showing and you merely cast to likely looking spots. The whole secret in dry-fly fishing is to make the fly drift naturally with the current without drag. For this, casting up and across stream is usually best. But there are times when you can cast downstream with plenty of slack in your line and float the fly to a waiting fish. On other occasions a dry fly like the spider can be pulled lightly to give it a skating action which induces a strike.

Wet flies are fished below the surface, and they represent drowned insects or flies which have submerged to lay eggs. Or fish may mistake them for hatching flies rising from the bottom of the stream as well as for other kinds of underwater food. Wet flies are tied on heavier wire hooks than dry flies and have soft hackles which pulse and breathe in the water. They should be sparsely tied with a minimum of hackle or feathers.

The standard wet fly or divided wing fly has one or two wings curved low over the body. They come in dark, somber, imitation colors or brighter, gaudier, attractor patterns. Other types of wet flies are the hairwing, featherwing, and hackle. Some of the wet-fly patterns which have been well tested are the Light Cahill, Quill Gordon, Iron Blue Dun, Gold Ribbed Hare's Ear, Royal Coachman, Leadwing Coachman, Professor, Brown Hackle, Gray Hackle Yellow, March Brown, Black Gnat, Mc-Ginty, Cowdung, Ginger Quill, and the Woolly Worm. With this assortment is sizes 8, 10, 12, and 14, you can fish in many parts of the country and catch fish. Naturally, there are local patterns and "special" flies which can be added to this list also.

The most common method of fishing a wet fly is to cast up and across stream and let it float with the current for most of the drift. When it is below, you start to retrieve it back in short jerks.

Nymphs represent the larvae of various forms of aquatic insects. The natural insects are found burrowing in the mud, hiding under stones, or in weeds. The majority of the nymphs found in streams and lakes consists of stone flies, May flies, dragon flies, and damsel flies. The nymphs of these are generally drab olive-green, brown, gray, or black in color with lighter yellowish bellies.

Nymph flies are constructed of various materials such as

hair, feathers, fur, wool, yarn, floss, rubber, plastic, wire, and lead in different combinations. The best ones try to imitate a specific nymph, but some are composites which can be mistaken by the fish for several kinds of nymphs. These flies are often weighted to make them sink faster.

Some of the more popular patterns of nymphs are the Stone fly, May fly, Caddis, Hendrickson, March Brown, Ginger Quill, Breadcrust, Dark Olive, Black Nymph and Dragonfly Nymph. Most nymphs are tied on hook sizes from 6 to 16, and it is best to get them from a professional local fly tier who copies the species most abundant in the waters you plan to fish.

Nymphs are effective for trout throughout the fishing season but are especially deadly in the early spring. They are also effective when trout are bulging or feeding on nymphs rising to the surface to hatch into adult flies, and they are used when fish are lying deep near the bottom and refuse to move. The most popular way to fish them is to cast upstream and let the current carry the nymph along. Slack line must be taken up, and the nymph is kept free from drag. Different levels should be tried when fishing nymphs since they work sometimes at the surface, other times a few inches under it, and still other times down deep near the bottom.

Although streamers and bucktails are also called "flies," they resemble minnows more than insects. They are long and are tied on long-shanked hooks. The name "bucktail" is usually given to those with wings of hair. The bodies are generally silver or gold tinsel. The hair is usually white, brown, yellow, red, green, blue, or combinations. Some of the most popular bucktail patterns are the Mickey Finn, Edson Tiger Light, Edson Tiger Dark, Professor, Silver Doctor, Black-nosed Dace, Brown and White, Black and White, and Yellow and White.

The name "streamer" is applied to those having long feather wings also tied on a long-shanked hook. The body materials may be silk, wool, peacock herl, chenille, or tinsel. Popular streamer patterns include the Black Ghost, Gray Ghost, Green Ghost, Montreal, Supervisor, Black and White, Yellow and White, White Marabou, Black Marabou, and Yellow Marabou.

Streamers and bucktails come tied on long-shanked hooks in sizes from No. 1/0 down to 12. The smaller ones are best for small streams and small trout, while the larger ones are used on big waters for big trout, bass, or other large fish.

When fish are chasing or feeding on minnows, the streamers and bucktails are most effective. But they can be fished any time for big trout which feed much of the time on minnows and other small fish. Streamers are good early in the year and later in the summer. They work best in the morning, evening, or after a recent rain. Streamers and bucktails are retrieved in short jerks and pauses to make them look like a darting or crippled minnow. They can be cast across stream, allowed to drift, and then retrieved in jerks. Or you can cast downstream and work and hold them in the current.

There are also flies which are tied to represent land insects rather than aquatic species. Called "terrestrials," they are tied to imitate spiders, worms, caterpillars, ants, beetles, grasshoppers, crickets, and similar land insects. It pays to carry an assortment of such flies, especially for summer and early fall fishing, when land insects are numerous and may form the bulk of the food supply of trout and bass.

Then there are the salmon flies, which are specially tied for these grand fish. Of course, many of the standard trout wet and dry patterns will take these fish on many occasions. They should be tied on the larger and heavier wire hooks than those used on regular trout flies. But there are many old tried and true salmon patterns which continue to catch these fish, and most anglers stick to such favorites. Popular wet flies are the Durham Ranger, Dusty Miller, Jock Scott, Silver Doctor, Silver Gray, Silver Wilkinson, Green Highlander, March Brown, Black Dose, Lady Amherst, Thunder and Lightning, Cosse-

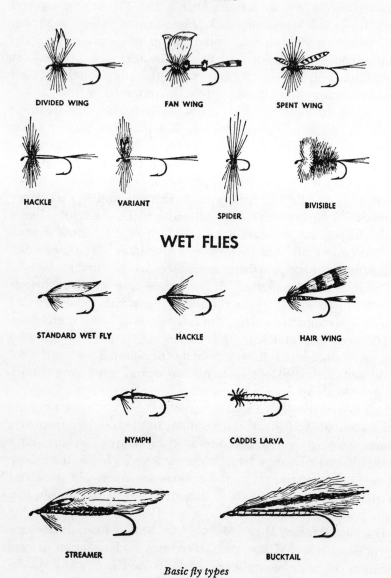

DRY FLIES

DIVIDED WING   FAN WING   SPENT WING

HACKLE   VARIANT   BIVISIBLE

SPIDER

WET FLIES

STANDARD WET FLY   HACKLE   HAIR WING

NYMPH   CADDIS LARVA

STREAMER   BUCKTAIL

Basic fly types

boom, Teagle Bee, and Mar Lodge. These may be tied on hook sizes from No. 12 up to 4/0 or 5/0. The larger sizes are best early in the season, while the smaller sizes work better later in the year when the water is low and clear. Good sizes for general salmon fishing are the flies tied on No. 4, 6, or 8 hooks.

Salmon will also take dry flies on many waters, especially late in the season when the water is low and clear. Many of the standard trout patterns tied on larger, stronger hooks can be used for this fishing. Some of the best dry-fly patterns for salmon are the Pink Lady, Rat Faced McDougall, Quill Gordon, Black Gnat, and the different spiders, bivisibles, and Wulff flies.

Finally we have the various flies and bugs used for black bass with the fly rod. Most of the standard trout patterns of wet and dry flies will also catch black bass. But they should be used in the larger sizes with stronger, heavier hooks. Trout streamers and bucktails in the larger sizes can also be used for black bass. There are also special bass wet flies which are tied on No. 1/0 or 2/0 hooks and are used alone or in combination with spinners. These include such patterns as the Colonel Fuller, Lord Baltimore, Royal Coachman, Brown Hackle, Gray Hackle, Yellow Sally, Professor, and Black Gnat.

The bass bugs are very deadly lures for black bass in the larger sizes and for big trout and panfish in the smaller sizes. Bass bugs are usually made of cork, balsa, plastic, or hair bodies and have feather or hair wings and tails. They are made to imitate such creatures as moths, beetles, mice, frogs, minnows, and small fish. There are many types on the market, and they come in various sizes and colors. One of the most popular types is the popper, which has an angled or cupped head and a tail of feathers or hair. Another good bass bug is the hairfrog, which has a body of hair and four tufts of hair resembling legs. Still another type is the bass bug with a bullet-shaped head and feather tail, which resembles a minnow more than a bug. Then we have the smaller poppers and bugs with flexible rubber legs, which are good for small bass and panfish. The bass bug angler should have a good assortment of these, but they should be chosen not only because of their appearance or action in the water but also on how they cast. Some of the most attractive bass bugs are very difficult to cast and are almost worthless. Bass bugs are worked in the water according to what they are supposed to represent. A moth-type bug should lie still and then move very slowly in quivering wriggles. A frog should move a few feet, then stop and rest. A minnow-type bass bug should be retrieved in short, darting movements.

There are also weighted flies, streamers, and bass bugs which are made for casting with spinning rods and reels rather than with a fly rod. These are similar to the lures of this type covered above, except that they have lead wire or other weight added so that they can be cast a fair distance.

One of the best all-around and deadliest lures used in fresh water is the spoon. It is among the oldest artificial lures used in commercial and sport fishing. It was used around 3000 B.C. and probably originated much earlier. The South Sea natives have been catching fish for thousands of years on pearl wobblers. And in the Scandinavian countries spoon-type lures were used 150 years ago and earlier.

Today spoons are even more popular and come in many sizes, shapes, weights, and materials. But they are usually stamped out of brass, copper, stainless steel, or other metal and are either polished, plated, or painted. The majority are silver or chrome in finish; but gold, brass, copper, and painted spoons are widely used.

Most spoons are oval in shape and are dished out to form concave and convex sides. But others are curved like an S or bent in the front or rear. They also have different outlines or shapes, with many of them imitating a small minnow or fish.

Most spoons have a "wobbling," swaying, or erratic darting action which is attractive to many fresh-water fish.

The well-known "Dardevle" spoon made by the Lou Eppinger Co., sold now for over fifty years, is a good example of a typical spoon. Many imitations of this shape are now found on the market.

Most spoons have free-swinging or fixed hooks attached. The smaller types usually have small double or treble hooks, while the larger ones may have single hooks. The hooks may be plain, or they may have feathers or bucktail tied around them. Some spoons also have weed guards attached.

The smallest spoons, weighing from $\frac{1}{16}$ to $\frac{1}{4}$ oz., are used with ultra-light and light spinning outfits. Some of the lightest can even be used with fly rods. They are best for trout, small bass, and panfish. The spoons weighing from $\frac{1}{4}$ to $\frac{3}{4}$ of an ounce are best for all-around use with spinning and casting outfits. They will take big trout, bass, pickerel, small pike, and muskies. The larger spoons, weighing from $\frac{3}{4}$ to 2 oz. or more, are used for casting and trolling for large fish such as big bass, lake trout, pike, muskies, and Pacific Salmon. These may run up to 4 or 5 in. in length and are equipped with heavy hooks.

Spoons are usually cast and reeled in slowly. They will take fish when reeled or trolled straight but are more appealing when jerked and allowed to sink and flutter, the process being repeated during the entire retrieve. This imitates a wounded or crippled minnow or small fish. Different depths are tried until the fish are located.

Spinners are similar to spoons in that they depend on flash to attract fish. In addition, they also give off vibrations which may play an important part in their effectiveness. Like spoons, spinners come in different sizes, shapes, weights, and finishes. The silver or chrome finish is the most popular, with gold, copper, brass, and painted finishes right behind.

Spinners generally have an oval or elongated leaf-shaped

blade. But other types may be round, kidney, or propeller-shaped. Spinners are made to spin or revolve on a wire shaft or on swivels. They may have no extra weights when used for trolling; but for casting they usually have metal heads, keels, or body forms, which add weight. There may be one, two, or as many as six or more blades used in tandem on spinners. These multiple blade spinners are used mostly for trolling. Spinners may have a single hook, double hook, treble hook, or a tandem hook. They may be used in conjunction with flies, pork rind, rubber, plastic, bucktail, or feather skirts. Others have plain hooks for use with natural baits. The famous June Bug spinner, when used with live bait such as worms or minnows on the trailing hook or hooks, is deadly for black bass, walleyes, pike, or big panfish. This is a good type for slow, deep trolling.

For casting, the weighted spinners such as the French types have become very popular in recent years. They are usually made with short wire shafts on which one or more metal beads or metal body forms are added to provide weight. These spinners usually have a special heavier blade than those found on the regular types.

Another type which has become popular is the "cherry bobber" or "cherry drifter," which has a balsa wood body shaped like a teardrop on the wire shaft and a thin, light, spinner blade in front of the wood. The balsa wood body is usually painted red but may be some other color. This lure is used with a small weight on the leader to get it down close to the bottom. It is used a lot in the Pacific Northwest for salmon and steelhead but also works on other fresh-water species.

When we come to the plug, we have the most popular lures for fresh-water fishing. Plugs are made from wood or plastic bodies and have single, double, or treble hooks attached either singly or in series. A walk into any fishing tackle store reveals a wide variety of these fish catchers. You have a wide choice of sizes, shapes, colors, weights, and actions. These lures account for some of the biggest fish caught in fresh water.

Some plugs are made for surface fishing, others dive, while still others sink. Surface plugs have cupped heads, big metal lips, wings, propellers, and other devices for creating a disturbance which attracts fish. They are made to represent crippled minnows, small fish, frogs, mice, small birds, or similar animals. Surface plugs are most effective for shallow water or calm water fishing and when fish are actually feeding near the surface.

Underwater plugs come in two types: floating and diving or the sinking models. The floating and diving types include those with grooved heads cut at an angle and those with metal lips. Some of these have long metal lips which enable them to dive many feet below the surface. Others travel only a few inches below the surface. They usually lie on the surface but dive to the different depths when retrieved. These plugs usually have a wobbling, darting, or wriggling action. They work best in waters from a few feet to moderate depths.

The sinking plugs slowly settle to the bottom and when reeled or jerked slowly hold a certain depth. They are good when the fish are down deep near the bottom and can be reached only with such plugs rather than with the surface or diving types.

The majority of the plugs made in the past were for bait-casting and weighed from $1/2$ to $5/8$ oz. They are still good when used with bait-casting tackle or with the heavier type spinning or spin-casting outfits. The larger sized plugs may weigh from $5/8$ to 2 oz.; and these are used for pike, muskellunge, lake trout, or very big bass. They are used with bait-casting rods or heavy spinning rods.

With the advent of spinning tackle, many manufacturers came out with smaller, lighter versions of the various bait-casting size plugs as well as new, original types. There are many lures weighing from ⅛ to ½ oz. on the market. Plugs lighter than ⅛ oz. are also available for ultra-light spinning. Most of the smaller plugs designed for spinning will catch any of the fresh-water species.

Many expert anglers will agree that color isn't too important in a surface plug. Red and white or all white or yellow are as good as any colors since the angler can see his plug for quite a distance. But underwater plugs should imitate the colors of the foods found in the waters being fished. Thus lakes where shiners or other bright silvery minnows or fish are found call for a plug with silver scale finishes. Where the fish feed on panfish such as yellow perch or sunfish, plugs with yellow, orange, green, or red can be used. If you're trying to imitate a drab-colored darter, stone cat, or small bullhead, use brown or black plugs. If frogs are eaten by the fish, plugs with green and white predominating are usually best.

Plugs are excellent for day or night fishing. The fish are attracted by their "plopping," "gurgling," and other noises or commotion they make on the water. Most plugs produce results when reeled in straight at a slow or moderate speed. Surface plugs which pop or create a fuss are best when fished very slowly. Most crippled minnows, frogs, or mice do not swim without rests. They travel a few inches or feet, then stop, then move again, then stop, etc. Try to imitate this action with your surface plugs. One of the exceptions to this rule occurs when schools of fish are chasing minnows on the surface. Then a fast-moving torpedo-type plug will often take them.

Underwater plugs should be given a jerk at regular intervals to increase their effectiveness. Sometimes a pause, such as stopping the plug a second or two, then resuming the retrieve, does the trick.

Sinking plugs should be allowed to settle almost to the bottom. Then the plug should be twitched, reeled a few inches, then allowed to settle once again. The idea is to let a big, lazy bass or other fish see the lure and tease him into striking it. The hooks on such lures must be sharp to set them at the lightest strike.

In recent years fresh-water anglers have discovered jigs, which are an old favorite with salt-water anglers. These are the lures with heavy metal heads, usually molded from lead and a trailing hook. They have skirts tied around the hook of buck-tail, polar bear hair, feathers, nylon, rubber, or plastic. The heads are usually nickel or chrome or painted the same color as the hair or feathers. The jig may be all white, yellow, black, brown, red, or combinations of these colors. The eye to which the line is attached is found on top of the lead head, and the jig always rides with the hook facing up. This makes them ideal for bouncing on the bottom among rocks and snags where other lures such as spoons or plugs hang up quickly.

Jigs come in various sizes, shapes, and weights. For light spinning outfits and small fish, those weighing from $\frac{1}{32}$ to $\frac{1}{4}$ oz. are best. For all-around fishing, those weighing from $\frac{1}{4}$ to $\frac{1}{2}$ oz. are good, while for big fish, deep waters, and heavy tackle jigs weighing from $\frac{5}{8}$ to 1 oz. or more can be used. Jigs will catch black bass, walleyes, crappies, white bass, and other panfish. Even carp and catfish have been hooked on them at times.

Jigs can be used in very deep water by simply letting them down to the bottom, then making them dance up and down at regular intervals. In water of moderate depths you cast out and let the jig sink. When it hits bottom, you let it rest a second or two, then lift it slightly, then let it settle again. Keep bouncing it on the bottom slowly until you get an indication of a strike, at which time you set the hook. Jigs can also be cast into shallow water or retrieved just below the surface when fish are feeding near the top. Here you either retrieve steadily or work the jig by jerking it at regular intervals.

There are also various kinds of pork rind strips, chunks, and shapes on the market. Pork rind can be used alone or with other lures to catch many fresh-water species. Strips of pork rind used alone are worked like streamer flies in short jerks or long sweeps of the rod tip. A fly rod or long cane or glass still fishing pole is best for this.

Pork rind is also used on various lures such as plugs, spoons, spinners, and jigs to make them more attractive. There are various widths, lengths, and colors such as white, red, yellow, and black. It's always a good idea to buy a couple of jars of such pork rind strips and carry them in your tackle box.

Pork chunks are cut into different shapes, but most of them are imitations of frogs. The legs may consist of just the rind alone, while the front part has a thick body of fat left on it. The pork chunk can be used in natural white color, but it is also available in green. Pork chunk is best used with a weedless hook and fished on top of lily pads and among grasses where frogs are found.

Another pork lure which anglers have used successfully in recent years is the "black eel," which is a tapered, narrow strip of pork dyed black and used with one or two hooks. It may be anywhere from 5 to 9 in. in length, depending on the tackle you want to use with it. The black eels work best when allowed to sink to the bottom, then reeled painfully slowly and twitched just off the bottom or even dragged along the bottom. Sometimes the fish hit them hard, and the hook can be set immediately. But most of the time you have to let the fish take the eel in its mouth before you try to set the hook. Black pork eels come already cut and packed in jars in the various sizes for spinning and bait-casting.

Finally, we come to the many natural, lifelike imitations of natural baits which are made from soft rubber and plastic materials. Such lures have been made for many years, but it is only in the last few years or so that they have become very popular. Now you'll find a wide variety of such lures from which to choose. There are rubber and plastic imitations of various insects such as hellgrammites, nymphs, grasshoppers, crickets, beetles, and spiders. These are small and light in weight and have to be used with a fly rod or cast with a small sinker ahead of them.

Then there are the rubber and plastic imitations of such natural baits as crayfish, frogs, salamanders, eels, and minnows. The minnows usually have a lip or plate to give them a built-in action, and they can be reeled in. But the other baits usually must be jerked or twitched to give them action.

One of the biggest booms in recent years has been the manufacture of plastic worms. These are now available in various lengths, weights, and colors. There are natural colored worms like night crawlers; but they also come in black, white, yellow, cream, red, green, blue spotted, and in combinations.

The worms are sold plain in plastic bags in varying numbers. These can be hooked with a single hook, but you can also buy the plastic worms with two or three hooks already attached. Still other baits of this type come with spinners in front or metal jig heads to provide weight for casting and sinking. Some of the worms also have silver or gold metal bands. These plastic worms are usually used the same way as the black pork eels—bounced or twitched or dragged very slowly just off the bottom.

9

FRESH-WATER ACCESSORIES

Besides the rods, reels, lines, and lures, the fresh-water fisherman needs many accessories which help to make his fishing more comfortable, safer, and productive. Some of these may fall into the class of gadgets and are not absolutely necessary to catch fish. But others are essential and may play a big part in your fishing success. Even some of the so-called gadgets have occasions on which they are needed and nothing can take their place.

Take boots, waders, and clothes, for example. There are some spots and seasons when you can fish without boots or waders; but other spots demand that you wade out into a stream, river, or lake and often stand up to your knees or hips in cold water for long periods. Or you may have to wade to a certain spot to reach a distant fish or productive area. Clothes, too, can make or break a fishing trip. If you are comfortably dressed and have the proper waterproof jackets, parkas, and pants, you can often fish in rainy or stormy weather when other anglers without this foul-weather gear have to give up and pack in. This often means you can have good fishing which other anglers miss.

Every fresh-water angler should own a pair of boots unless he always fishes from a boat. The trout angler can use boots in shallow, small streams where the water isn't too deep. If you fish a lake which has swampy or marshy shores, boots will make it possible to walk in the mud without wetting your feet. And in shallow lakes or rivers you can wade out some distance from shore to reach deeper water when you cast.

There are many kinds of boots on the market, but make sure you get the special light types made for fishermen. The heavy work boots should be avoided. The light, all-rubber hip boots will serve the purpose for most shallow water fishing. For fishing cold waters, there are insulated type boots; but these are heavier if you must do a lot of walking. There are also short boots which come up to your ankles or knees. These are best for fishing from a boat or in the rain. They will keep your feet dry but aren't too cumbersome or heavy, and they can be removed quickly if you fall in the water or the boat overturns. Most boots have rubber cleats on their soles which hold well in mud and sand. But if you fish in rocky or mossy streams, boots with felt soles are better.

For deep wading in streams, rivers, and lakes, waist-high or chest-high waders are needed. Waders are made of various materials such as plastics, rubberized canvas, and rubber. Plastic waders are light and excellent for hot weather or when walking long distances. They can also be dried quickly by turning them inside out. They don't stand up as well around rocks as other heavier types and therefore aren't too durable on streams with rough rocky formations. They also wear out more quickly than heavier waders, and the angler who does a lot of fishing may need a new pair every year. But they are also less expensive than the heavier waders; and in the long run, even if you buy them more often, you still get your money's worth. Plastic waders also take up less room and can be rolled up and carried in a small space.

The heavier rubberized canvas or all-rubber waders are strong, durable, and are best for fishing in cold waters such as in the north, early spring, fall, or rainy, stormy weather. You can wear heavy underwear, pants, and woolen socks under them and fish in fair comfort under such conditions. These rubber waders are not too good for walking long distances, especially in hot weather. But they stand up well from wear and tear. Of the two kinds, the rubberized canvas waders are lighter than the all-rubber types. However, there are various weights of rubber waders on the market; and you can usually find a pair that is light enough for most of your fresh-water fishing.

Waders come mainly in two types: those with stocking feet and those with boot feet. The stocking foot waders require some kind of wading shoes or brogues which are worn over them. The boot foot waders are permanently attached to the rest of the wader. Boot foot waders are quicker to put on and remove and are preferred for deep cold waters where you don't do too much walking. The stocking foot waders are best for small trout streams and where you don't wade too deep or stay too long in cold water. They are also fine if you have to do considerable walking.

Most rubber foot waders come with rubber cleats and heels; and for fishing sandy areas, mud, gravel or pebble bottoms, and quiet waters, they will usually serve the purpose. But when used in deep, fast rivers and on slippery rocks, waders with felt soles are better and safer. If these are not attached permanently to the soles of your waders, you can have it done. However, felt-soled waders are expensive; and it's better to buy a pair of wading sandals with felt or hobnail soles. There are also many types of ice-creepers and chains which can be worn over waders or boots to insure a grip on slippery rocks.

For the stocking foot waders you need a pair of wading shoes or brogues. Some anglers wear nothing but a pair of high top sneakers or gym shoes. These are light but they have plain rubber soles which often slip, and they don't protect the feet as well as heavier or special wading shoes. You can get the wading shoes with rubber, felt, or hobnailed soles. The felt soles will work on many slippery surfaces, but they don't last too long. The hobnailed soles will also hold on most slippery rocks and last longer.

A jacket of some kind is also needed by the fresh-water angler when fishing from shore or a boat. In a boat an ordinary jacket will often serve the purpose. But for the trout, steelhead, or salmon angler who does a lot of wading, a special fishing vest is almost a must. These should have plenty of pockets for carrying flies and other lures, leaders, dressing, insect repellent, small angler's clip, and any of the other items required. It should also have large zippered pockets for fly boxes. Most of these vests also have extra large pockets in the back of the vest for carrying a sandwich or a raincoat. Some vests also have a flat creel which can be attached or detached at will. The best vest to get is one which is extra short so that it will clear the water when you wade in deep spots.

For rainy weather it's a good idea to carry waterproof gear. There are many light raincoats which will often do the trick to wait out a rain or for still-fishing. However, if you do a lot of walking or casting, a waterproof parka jacket with hood and pants to match are best. These are separate, and on cold days the jacket acts as a windbreaker. During rainy weather you can fish in comfort if you wear the jacket, pants, and a pair of short boots. The parka type jackets and pants come in light plastic materials or in heavier rubberized canvas styles. The nylon or neoprene jackets and pants are light, waterproof, and wear well.

A hat of some kind is needed to protect the hair, head, and eyes from rain and sun. You can, of course, use an old hat for this purpose; but there are special fishing hats which are light and water repellent. A cap with a long peak or visor offers good protection from the sun. On rainy days a waterproof hat with a wide brim offers protection, and this type can also be used on sunny days to protect the eyes, ears, and neck. It should be made of a light waterproof cloth material.

Fresh-water anglers also need containers for their different fishing lures, flies, sinkers, extra lines, reels, and other gear. The fly fisherman will find many transparent boxes which can be slipped into the pockets of his vest. These have separate compartments for holding the flies. There are also larger sizes, which can be used by boat fishermen. For carrying flies in large numbers, there are the fly books, which are usually made from leather or canvas and have felt or sheepskin linings. These are compact and serve for holding wet flies, nymphs, and streamers. For dry flies there are many different kinds of fly boxes made of plastic, aluminum, and other light metals. These have some type of clips or compartments for holding the flies. Those with separate compartments each having its own snap-up cover are best since you can open one at a time and the wind won't blow the flies away. And if you happen to over-turn the box, you won't lose all your flies.

For the shore fisherman there are many kinds of fishing bags such as canvas shoulder bags which can be worn and which will hold lures, reels, lines, sinkers, and even your lunch or extra clothing. They come in different sizes, but the smaller or medium-sized ones are best. Shoulder bags are handy if you must hike long distances and carry all your stuff with you. If you merely want something to hold your lures and a few accessories, a fishing vest made in the apron style is a good bet. These have many pockets for carrying lure boxes and other items.

The boat angler is better off with some sort of large tackle box which holds many lures and accessories. Nowadays they come in various sizes, styles, and materials such as steel, alumi-num, Fiberglas, plastic, or wood. These tackle boxes now come in different sizes for spinning, bait-casting, and combinations of the two. Usually the main difference between a tackle box

Four types of floats for spin fishing made by Dayton Bait Co.

Various types of floats and bobbers used in fresh-water fishing.

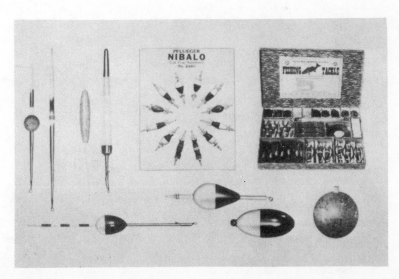

A collection of weighted flies, spinner-fly combinations, spinners, and other lures designed for ultra-light and light spinning. They are distributed by Continental Arms Corp.

South Bend Super-Duper lure comes in many sizes and finishes for fly rod, spinning, casting, and trolling.

South Bend Spin-I-Didee plug is a typical propeller type surface lure.

Arbogast Jitterbug is an old favorite e plug which comes in ⅝ and ¼ oz. sizes.

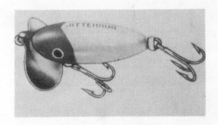

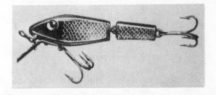

Kautzky's Lazy Ike plug comes in a wide variety of sizes, weights, and colors for use with any fresh-water tackle.

Mirrolure, a jointed underwater plug, in ¼, ½, ⅜, and ⁹⁄₁₆ oz. weights.

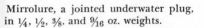

Fred Arbogast Arbo-Gaster comes in ¼ and ⅝ oz. sizes It floats and dives deep.

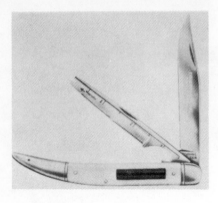

This Schrade-Walden Fisherman's Pal pocket knife has a scaler, disgorger, bottle opener, ruler, and hook sharpener.

Kennedy Stowaway tackle box is unique since it is designed with side drawers and can be used under a boat seat out of the way at all times.

Langley De-Liar scale weighs fish up to 8 lb. and is small and compact.

Red-Lok fish stringer has individual snaps on swivels which slide on chain.

Left: Hodgman Brighton coated rubber boot foot waders are popular during spring and fall and for cold water wading. *Right:* Cumberland fishing jackets and vests for fly fishermen have many pockets for holding flies and accessories.

These fishing bags, creels, caps, and tackle bag made by American Pad & Textile Co. fill many needs in fresh-water fishing.

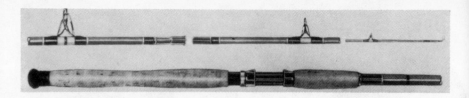

Wright & McGill Marauder ocean and boat spinning rod comes in 9 and 10 ft. lengths and is designed for yellowtail and albacore fishing as well as light surf fishing.

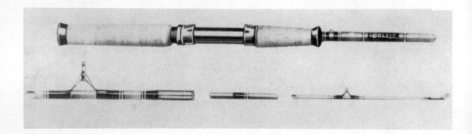

Garcia-Conolon light salt-water spinning rods for one-handed casting come in lengths from 6½ to 7 ft. and in various actions to handle lures from ¼ to 1½ oz.

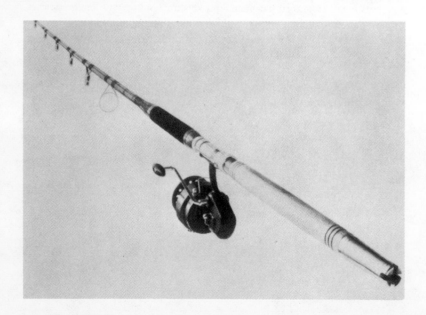

This Alcedo big-game trolling spinning rod made by Continental Arms Corp. is the first roller guide big-game rod constructed for use with a spinning reel. It has a swiveling roller tip-top.

The Mariner 55, sold by Rockland Tackle Co., weighs 15 oz. and holds 260 yds. of 10 lb. test line. It has ball bearings and a genuine agate roller.

The Orvis 100 reel is popular with salt-water anglers for use with one-hand spinning rods. It holds 190 yd. of 8 lb. test line and weighs 10 oz.

Ru-Pacific salt-water spinning reel has the finger type pick-up and holds 200 yd. of 20 lb. test line. It is imported by J. M. P. R. Trading Corp.

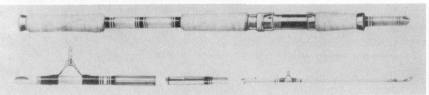

Garcia Conolon Companion surf rod is 9 ft. long, comes in two sections, and can cast lures from 1 to 4 oz. in weight.

The Fin-Nor salt-water spinning reel comes in two sizes and has a pick-up arm, machined gears, and full circle disc drag.

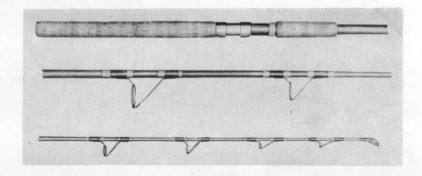

Continental-Alcedo heavy duty surf rod has a light cork hanlle and grip and special non-fouling guides.

Pfleuger 9 ft. two piece spinning rod is suitable for light and medium surf spinning.

made for spinning and one made for bait-casting is in the over-all size of the box and the compartments. Spinning tackle boxes are usually smaller and have smaller compartments because the lures are not as big as the bait-casting types. Some tackle boxes have movable partitions for the trays or compartments which you can shift around to accommodate different sized lures.

For the casual angler one of the combination spinning-bait-casting tackle boxes of medium size will usually fill the bill. Here you can keep both spinning lures and the larger bait-casting lures in the different sized compartments. Those who do a lot of fishing and take along many lures may want a separate big box for spinning lures and another big box for bait-casting lures.

Most of the tackle boxes have cantilever trays, numbering anywhere from two to ten, which swing out when the box is opened. The cantilever mechanism should work smoothly and be sturdy. The same goes for the hinges, handle, and lock. Examine these for sturdiness and for the weight of the metal stock and plating. Some tackle boxes have inferior hardware parts which do not operate efficiently or may break or wear out soon. When it comes to tackle boxes, it's smart to buy a good one. They last a long time, and too many anglers suffer for years with a small, tinny, troublesome tackle box when a few dollars more would have given them the best there is.

For landing or boating a fish, a landing net or gaff is required. The angler fishing a small stream for trout and bass can use one of the smaller nets which are worn on the person. Many of these are light and have elastic rubber attached to the handle. Some are made of wood, while others have light metal frames and handles. For landing fish from a boat, you need a landing net with a wider hoop and longer handle. Many sizes are available, and the light aluminum types with detachable handles are convenient. If you do a lot of fishing for salmon,

muskellunge, big pike, or carp, you may find a gaff more practical. These also come in various lengths and sizes. The hook
should be of strong steel and be fairly large at the gap. For
Atlantic salmon, a Lee Wulff salmon tailer captures the fish
without harming it and is safer to carry than a gaff.

After you land or boat your fish, you have to keep them alive
or at least fresh. Fish stringers and creels of various kinds are
on the market for this purpose. The wading fisherman who
fishes a small stream for trout or bass will find a willow creel one
of the best for preserving fish. If this is too bulky for your taste,
you can always get a lighter type creel made from matting,
canvas, or plastic. These lie flat against your body and don't
interfere with your casting or movements.

The shore fisherman will find a cotton cord or chain fish
stringer useful. A fish bag can also be used, and there are many
net-type bags which can be bought. The boat angler can also
use such stringers or bags if the boat doesn't have a built-in
fish well. The stringers are usually made from a strong cord or
chain. The chain type stringers with safety pin snaps are very
quick and easy to use. A fish pierced through the lower lip will
live for a long time in the water.

The fresh-water fisherman should also have some kind of
knife with him to take care of the various cutting tasks that
arise on almost every fishing trip. One of the best knives for
this purpose is a pocket knife made especially for fishermen.
The stainless steel type with a long blade, fish scaler, hook disgorger, bottle opener, and hook sharpener is the one to get.
And don't buy a cheap one for $1.98. They are almost worth-
less. Spend at least $5.00 for such a knife, and it will hold a
sharp edge for a long time and give you years of service. It can
even be used to clean and fillet fish in a pinch. But for this purpose a good fillet knife is better. It should have a sharp edge and
long, thin blade. Some of them also have saw edges on one side

for scaling, but a regular fish scaler is cheap and usually best for this work.

A handy gadget for the fly fisherman as well as other anglers is the angler's clip. This is a combination tool which has a stiletto, disgorger, leader, or line cutter and is attached to a loop cord.

A good pair of pliers is also handy to have along on a fishing trip. If you haven't a pair of combination pliers, it's a good idea to carry two pairs—one with a cutting edge and another with a gripping nose. Cutting pliers should be sharp and strong enough to cut through the heaviest wire hooks that you are using. In an emergency they are invaluable when a hook gets caught in any part of your body. A pair of long-nosed gripping pliers is useful in removing hooks from a fish's mouth.

To be prepared for many emergencies, a tool kit can also be taken along. This can have, besides the pliers, a file, small hammer, small saw which cuts wood and metal, some screwdrivers, and any other tools which you may need. Of course, you may not be able to carry this around with you; but it's a good idea to have it in the boat or at least in the car. The same goes for a first-aid kit of some sort to take care of minor cuts and injuries.

To protect your face and hands from the sun, a sun-tan lotion is helpful. Sun glasses are also a must to protect your eyes, and Polaroid types help in locating fish below the surface of the water.

During the summer months and in tropical climes an insect repellent is something you need if you want to fish in peace, especially at dusk or at night.

An oil can, reel grease, and small sharpening stone are needed for lubricating reels and for sharpening hooks and knives.

The angler who fishes with live bait will need a minnow bucket or bait can to carry and keep such natural baits alive.

There are many kinds of minnow buckets of the floating type which can be used from a boat or shore. Still others have inner liners which breathe and permit air to enter to keep the water fresh and cool. Bait containers are made of wood, metal, plastics, and fiber materials for keeping worms, crickets, grasshoppers, and other baits alive for long periods.

Finally, we have such items as stream thermometers, scales for weighing fish, searchlights or headlights, rod cases, reel cases, and thermos bottles and picnic bags, which also belong on many fishing trips.

10

SALT-WATER SPINNING RODS

One thing that the spinning reel did for salt-water fishing in a big way was to introduce light tackle fishing to thousands of anglers. Before spinning, most of the tackle used in salt-water fishing was on the heavy side. Rods were still like clubs, reels bulky and heavy, and the lines were thick and strong. When spinning tackle came along, many salt-water anglers tried it and soon discarded their heavy conventional outfits. Today vast numbers of salt-water anglers are enjoying light tackle fishing with added sport, fun, and strangely enough—more and bigger fish. Spinning tackle has made it possible to hook and land many more wary fish such as bonefish, snook, sea trout, striped bass, channel bass, yellowtail, albacore, bonito, and many other species. Those who seek the ultimate in sport are even going after big, heavy, offshore fish such as sailfish, marlin, and sharks with spinning outfits.

It wasn't too long ago that the angler who wanted to try salt-water spinning had to use fresh-water rods and reels. Or he had only a few salt-water models from which to choose. Most of these were on the light side, and there wasn't much of a variety to pick from. But there's a big difference today! Now we have salt-water rods to take care of almost every kind of spin fishing.

Of course, there's no harm in trying your fresh-water tackle in salt water, provided it's used for light fishing and you don't have to cast heavy sinkers or lures. But in the long run, it is better to get a rod designed especially for salt-water fishing. Such rods have the backbone and are made of heavier parts and non-corrosive fittings.

As with fresh-water spinning rods, hollow glass rods are also favored for most salt-water spinning rods, especially if any kind of casting is required and you want to cut down on the weight of the rod as much as possible. You can't beat a hollow glass rod for all-around fishing performance. However, there are uses for solid glass rods, too, in bottom fishing and trolling. If made too long or too thick, the solid glass rods tend to get too heavy.

There are also a few salt-water spinning rods made from split bamboo being sold and used. These are fine if they are well made and designed for salt-water fishing. The best rods of this type should be made from split-bamboo sections that are impregnated with some substance which waterproofs the wood and makes it impervious to heat, cold, humidity, or water. The Orvis impregnated rods are in this class and are permanized with a bakelite resin to make them strong, tough, and durable. Such rods are not affected by moisture like ordinary bamboo, which may rot and weaken.

All the metal fittings on a salt-water spinning rod should be of non-corrosive material. Such parts as the reel seat, ferrules, and guides should not rust or corrode when used in salt water.

The guides on salt-water spinning rods should be wrapped on firmly with thread and should have several coats of varnish or other protective coating. Test the guides to make sure that they are not loose. A slight amount of play can't be avoided with some types of guides; but if it is too loose, it can get out of line or work off. Some of the cheaper rods do not have enough varnish on the thread holding the guides. If you buy such a rod, it's a good idea to add two or three more coats of varnish over the wrappings.

The guides on salt-water spinning rods take more wear than

those on fresh-water rods. This is especially true of the tip guide, where the reeling in of heavy lures or the playing of big fish creates friction and wear, which may soon cut grooves in soft metal. So it's a good idea to buy a rod with hard metal tip-top guides. Some of these are equipped with genuine agate guides, and these are hard and durable; but care must be taken not to crack or break them.

The first guide nearest the reel on a salt-water spinning rod is usually of an extra large diameter to narrow down the spiralling coils of line which leave the reel. On some of the longer, heavier, salt-water spinning rods these guides may be 2½ to 3 in. in diameter. The guides on the rod should graduate in size progressively to smaller ones toward the tip, and there should be enough guides to distribute the strain evenly along the entire length of the rod.

The reel seat on most salt-water rods made today is the locking screw type, which holds the reel securely in place. The better reel seats of this type have two screw locks, which are less apt to work loose than a single one. When you buy a salt-water spinning rod, make sure that the reel you have will fit the reel seat on the rod. There are so many different reels and rods on the market that they often vary in the size and thickness of the reel foot. Reel seats also vary in the space allotted for holding the reel foot. So try fitting the spinning reel on the rod before you buy it. It should lock securely in place, and when tightened the reel should not move or shift position.

To simplify matters we can divide salt-water spinning rods into three classes: light, medium, and heavy. The light salt-water spinning rod is very similar to the heavy fresh-water models. In fact, you can use your heavy fresh-water rod for light salt-water fishing. Or you can use the light salt-water rod in fresh water. The guides on a salt-water rod may be somewhat larger and stronger than those found on fresh-water rods because you may want to change to a larger salt-water spinning reel at times. Another difference is that the lower grip or handle is often longer on the salt-water rod. This is a big aid when working lures such as surface plugs or jigs. The handle can rest against your forearm and saves your wrist. The longer handle is also less tiring when you are fighting a fish for any length of time. You can rest it against your leg or groin to give your arm and wrist a rest.

The light salt-water rod should be short enough and light enough to cast with one hand. This means that the 6, 6½, and 7 ft. lengths are best for this work. Some of the rods in this class will handle lures up to 1½ oz., but most of them are made to cast lures up to 1 oz. or so. And when used with thin lines, they can cast the lighter lures a fair distance. This makes the light salt-water rod a very practical tool. For most fishing situations an 8 lb. test line is best with such a rod. But you can use a 6 lb. test for light lures and a 10 or 12 lb. test for heavier lures and bigger fish.

The light spinning rod is ideal for boat fishing in bays, sounds, rivers, and offshore for small fish. It can also be used from shore in the quieter waters. Such a rod is popular for wading and fishing in Florida, the Bahamas, the Gulf of Mexico, and other shallow flats and protected waters. For such fish as small striped bass, bluefish, sea trout, weakfish, snook, small channel bass, and salmon, the light rod is effective and sporty. It is also the best rod to use if you do a lot of jigging with bucktail jigs or diamond jigs for the smaller fish in shallow waters.

The light rod can also be used for light trolling and bottom fishing in shallow waters where currents and tides aren't too strong. You can't use sinkers much heavier than 2 or 3 oz. with such a rod. The best reels to use with the light rods are the fresh-water models or the smaller salt-water types.

The medium salt-water spinning rods run from about 7 to 10 ft. in over-all length. These rods have a butt or handle anywhere from 14 to 22 in. long and are cast with two hands. The

shorter, lighter rods in this class make good small boat rods.
The longer, heavier ones are used from party boats and for surf
fishing. In this class you'll find many of the steelhead and
salmon rods used for drift fishing in the rivers. The longer 9 ft.
models are widely used for "mooching" for salmon in the
Northwest. The medium weight rods can usually handle lures
up to 2½ oz. and somewhat heavier sinkers. Lines testing
from 10 to 20 lb. are generally used with these rods. The
medium salt-water spinning rods can also be used for pier, dock,
bridge, and jetty fishing with the lighter lures and sinkers for
the smaller fish. They can be used for bottom fishing with light
sinkers or for trolling in shallow waters. In other words, the
rods in this class are versatile tools which can take care of many
fishing situations from shore or boat.

The heavy salt-water spinning rods may run from 8½ to 15
ft. in over-all length. Many of these rods are used for surf fishing, and these are covered in Chapter 12. But other rods in this
class are also suitable for use for shore, pier, dock, or boat fishing. On the West Coast, for example, the heavy spinning rods
in lengths from 9 to 12 ft. are preferred for "live bait" and
jig fishing from the Southern California party boats for albacore, yellowtail, and small tuna.

In the heavy spinning rod class you'll also find the offshore
spinning rods, which are used in trolling for sailfish, marlin,
tuna, swordfish, and sharks. A special rod of this type with
roller guides and swiveling roller tip-top has been made by the
tackle division of the Continental Arms Corp. of New York.
This rod also has a heavy duty big-game locking reel seat and
solid wood butt. It also has a slotted butt cap which fits into the
gimbal of a fishing chair.

The construction of the heavy spinning rod varies according to the manufacturer. Some rods have heavy hardwood butts
and heavy brass chrome-plated reel seats. Other rods have
lighter hollow glass butt sections with light aluminum reel seats

and cork grips. This makes a somewhat lighter rod without much loss of strength. In fact, some of the strongest rods of this class are made from one-piece hollow glass blanks. Other rods are made from one-piece tip sections fitted into a separate butt section. For heavy fishing, the big-game type reel seats which have a screw lock and slotted ferrule which holds the tip section securely is best. Still other heavy rods are made in two pieces with a ferrule in the middle. These, of course, are easier to store or transport by air, car, or train. But the ferrules should be extra strong and securely fitted to stand the strain of casting or fighting a big fish.

Salt-water spinning rods have come a long way since the first ones were tried in this country right after World War II. Now there are light outfits suitable for the smallest and wariest fish as well as heavy outfits capable of handling many of the big-game fishes formerly caught only on conventional rods and reels.

11
SALT-WATER SPINNING REELS

When spinning first became popular in this country, the first reels of this type used in salt-water fishing were the small fresh-water models. Then, a short time later, larger special salt-water reels were imported from abroad. American manufacturers soon began making larger spinning reels designed especially for salt-water fishing. Now you have a wide choice of imported and domestic salt-water spinning reels.

Actually, any spinning reel made for fresh water can also be used for salt-water fishing. In fact, many such reels are being used in salt water, especially with light spinning rods. There's nothing wrong with this if you confine your fishing to the smaller species and don't use heavy lures or sinkers. But many fresh-water reels can't take it when exposed to salt water and the rough fishing practiced in the ocean. They don't stand up, and the parts give out or fail to work properly. Other fresh-water reels corrode badly. Still others are too small to hold enough line in the heavier strengths. So in the long run it's better to use a spinning reel specially designed for salt-water fishing. Even then, you should pick the correct size for the fishing you plan to do.

Salt-water spinning reels come in various sizes and weights from about 10 oz. on up to 26 oz. for the heavier big-game models. For convenience we can divide them into three classes:

light, medium, and heavy. The light salt-water spinning reels weigh from about 8 to 12 oz. and are used for light fishing and light lures and lines. Many such reels are actually fresh-water reels used in salt-water since only a few reels of this size are designed especially for salt-water fishing. These light salt-water spinning reels hold anywhere from 150 to 300 yd. of 6, 8 or 10 lb. test line. The light spinning reels are usually used with one-handed spinning rods for boat and shore fishing.

The medium salt-water spinning reels weigh from about 12 to 20 oz., have larger spools, stronger parts, and gears, and are used to cast heavier weights. Such reels will hold anywhere from 150 to 400 yd. of line testing from 12 to 25 lb., which are the sizes of lines usually used with these reels. The reels in this class are used from boats, piers, bridges, shore, or surf for various kinds of fish. Because they hold more line than the smaller salt-water spinning reels, they are popular for use with the two-handed spinning rods when fishing from boats or surf, especially if casting is required.

The heavy salt-water spinning reels weigh from 20 to 26 oz. and have extra-large spools, heavy-duty parts, and gears. These include the largest salt-water reels made today. They may hold anywhere from 250 to 800 yards of line testing from 15 to 40 lb. Such reels are designed for the heaviest surf fishing and long casts as well as for offshore or big-game fishing.

Salt-water spinning reels have the same features found on fresh-water spinning reels such as drags, line pick-ups, anti-reverse, interchangeable spools, etc. Naturally the parts are usually larger, stronger, and more durable than those on fresh-water reels. They have to be able to take the sudden or prolonged strain of casting and working heavy lures and fighting big fish, not to mention the wear and tear of sand, salt water, and strain when used for surf or offshore fishing. Any salt-water spinning reel which is made of cheap or inferior materials or poorly constructed shows up these defects quickly under actual fishing conditions.

A good salt-water spinning reel is made of materials which are highly resistant to the corrosive action of salt water. Various metal alloys and plastics are used for this purpose, and various finishes and platings are also used to further protect the metals from corrosion or rust. Some reels are better than others in this respect; but most of them require care such as washing in fresh water, cleaning, and oiling to prevent corrosion and rust.

In choosing a salt-water spinning reel, the drag or friction clutch is an important consideration. With fresh-water reels you can often get away with using drags which jerk or bind, especially for the smaller species which rarely run or take much line. But in salt-water fishing you never know when you might hook one of the bigger, faster moving species. Some of these such as the bonefish, tarpon, barracuda, yellowtail, albacore, bonito, striped bass, and channel bass will rip off many yards of line at a fast clip, not to mention the heavier fish such as tuna, sailfish, marlin, and swordfish, which can take hundreds of feet of line at a terrific speed. When you're going after such fish, a smooth, constant drag is a must.

The drag on your reel can be set as described in Chapter 2. However, you will find it necessary to change your drag setting more often in salt water than in fresh. The fish run bigger, vary more in size and have tougher jaws. In addition, you often have to contend with heavy surf, strong currents, and tides. For example, when fishing with small, light lures and tiny hooks, you can often use a light drag to hook a fish. The same goes for fish with soft mouths. Yet when you change to lures which are larger and have bigger hooks, you may need a tighter drag to drive home the hooks. This is especially true of fish with tough jaws and mouths.

When fishing for fish which start off on long, fast runs as soon as hooked, you need a fairly light drag. If a fish takes a lot of line, you may have to loosen the drag still more. On the other hand, when you have a fish near the boat or shore ready for boating or landing, you often have to tighten the drag in order to bring him in. This is especially true when beaching a fish in the surf or when fishing in a strong tide or current. Of course, you should never tighten the drag so much that it risks breaking the line.

There are times, too, when bottom fishing from a boat, pier, bridge, or shore for small species which have to be brought in quickly or lifted some distance, when a very tight drag is required. This can be done with the heavier lines. But when fishing for the larger gamefish, the drag setting should always be well below the breaking strength of the line. A sudden leap or run can always be expected until the fish is completely licked or boated.

Salt-water spinning reels with full bail pick-ups are the most common at the present time. A good working full bail is a pleasure to use and is preferred by those casting artificial lures from small boats, shore, or surf. Such lures as metal spoons, metal squids, and other fast sinking lures often have to be reeled back almost the instant they hit the water. With a manually operated pick-up, there's a split second or so before the line is caught and the retrieve is started. This often means that the lure sinks a couple of feet, and in rocky or weedy areas this means a fouled lure.

However, reels with bail or finger pick-ups often cause trouble when they are bent out of shape or springs break or weaken or the line tangles around the pick-up arm or finger. So some anglers prefer a manual type pick-up because they always work and won't let an angler down during a crucial moment. Some spinning reel manufacturers also recommend using the manual pick-up when heavy lures are being cast with their reels. This is often the case when the return spring of the automatic bail pick-up isn't strong enough to close the bail against the heavy outgoing lures. Some reels are made so that they can be converted from full bail to manual pick-up by simply removing the wire bail. This provides an added insurance of being able to keep on fishing in case something goes wrong with the bail pick-up.

The roller on salt-water spinning reels should be made of some hard substance such as sapphire, genuine agate, hard chrome, or other tough metal which resists wear and grooving. If the roller is supposed to turn, it should do so freely. Rollers made of soft metal quickly wear and groove when an angler is using heavy lures or fighting big fish.

Most salt-water spinning reels have an anti-reverse lock, and this is even more important in salt-water fishing than in fresh-water. Most anglers fishing with bait and sinker on the bottom leave the anti-reverse in the "on" position at all times so that they can remove their hand from the reel handle. If you use your salt-water spinning reel for trolling, you should also leave the anti-reverse on most of the time. The same thing holds true if you are jigging with a bucktail lure diamond jig. Some surf anglers using artificial lures leave the anti-reverse in the "off" position while casting and retrieving and turn it on only when a fish is hooked. Others prefer to fish all the time with the anti-reverse in the "on" position. And, of course, the anti-reverse should be left in the "on" position when the rod and reel is being carried from one spot to another.

Spools and spool capacity are also important in salt-water spinning reels. The spools must be strong enough to take the strain of fighting a big fish. Nylon lines, especially monofilament, when packed tight on a reel spool during a fight with a fish, exert a lot of pressure and may break a weak spool.

The spool should hold enough line for the fishing you plan to do. For small species of fish and light fishing, this is no problem; and most of the salt-water spinning reels hold enough line. But when surf fishing where long casts are required, you need the larger reels with big spools. You won't get much distance in your casts if you use a small spool and heavy line. As soon as your line falls too far below the flange of the spool, your cast is stopped short. The larger diameter, wider spools help to overcome this; and you get more distance.

For offshore fishing you also need the larger spinning reels with big spools to hold plenty of line. With more and more heavy-duty salt-water spinning reels being made and the new lines with thinner diameters, the problem of enough line on the spool is being solved for most fishing situations encountered in salt-water fishing.

One important consideration when buying a salt-water spinning reel is the availability of spare parts and repair service. Make certain that the manufacturer or distributor of the reel is still in business and that the reel can be repaired at tackle stores or the factory. Salt-water spinning reels often require new parts or repairs, and these should be available without too much delay. Some of the manufacturers and distributors provide quicker repair service than others. A few even make a practice of repairing within forty-eight hours most reels sent to them.

The care given a salt-water spinning reel will determine how long it will last and how well it will operate. The reel should be washed in fresh running water after being used in salt water. It should be wiped with a damp cloth if you don't want to rinse it under the faucet. Then it can be wiped dry and oiled at all friction points such as the handle knob, the roller, each end of the bail pick-up, etc. This is best done after and before each fishing trip.

About once each season, the reel can be taken apart and the gears can be cleaned with gasoline or kerosene. Then it should be repacked with the special grease made for spinning reels.

Do not monkey with the gears and drag washers, springs, or other complicated parts unless you are certain you know what you are doing. If anything goes wrong with the reel, take it to a tackle store specializing in such repairs or send it back to the factory. If you do a lot of fishing, your reel may require over-hauling every year or two. And it's also a good idea to buy two reels just in case something goes wrong with one of them. Then you have a spare reel which can be used in such an emergency.

12
SPINNING SURF RODS AND REELS

The spinning rod and reel have done a lot to make surf fishing popular with the average angler. It often takes years to become an expert caster with a conventional rod and reel. But with spinning tackle, almost anyone can learn how to cast a good distance in the surf after a few trips to the beach.

When spinning tackle was first introduced into this country, surf anglers went for it in a big way. The spinning reel solved the backlash headache which had plagued conventional surf tackle users for a century. Most of the spinning reels first introduced were for fresh-water fishing, and surf anglers had trouble finding long or powerful spinning rods or reels big enough for surf fishing. However, it wasn't long before larger reels were imported and American companies started making bigger reels and longer, more powerful rods designed for surf fishing.

The modern surf angler can now find almost any length and action he wants in a surf spinning rod. In the beginning surf anglers had to use light lures and lines because the rods and reels weren't big enough or strong enough to handle the heavier lures and lines. Now, however, with the latest surf spinning rods and reels, you can cast almost all weights and sinkers right up to the heaviest used in practical surf fishing.

Spinning surf rods or outfits can be divided into three classes:

light, medium, and heavy. Light spinning rods will run from about $7\frac{1}{2}$ to $9\frac{1}{2}$ ft. in over-all length. The butt on such a rod will be long enough so that you can cast with two hands. Such a rod will have a fairly limber action and will be able to handle the lighter lures and sinkers. This will include the smallest lures used for surf fishing, usually weighing from about 1 oz. up to 2 oz. Lines testing from 10 to 12 lb. are used with this light outfit. Such an outfit will not be very good for bait fishing except for the smaller fish found in the surf and when conditions permit using light 2 or 3 oz. sinkers. Such a surf spinning rod is ideal for school stripers, small bluefish, weakfish, northern and southern whiting, and croakers.

The medium weight surf spinning outfit will have a rod running from 8 to 10 ft. in over-all length. The butt section of such a rod will range from 18 to 26 in. in length. Such a rod will cast lures weighing from 1 to 3 oz., which will include most of the lures used in surf fishing. Lines testing from 12 to 20 lb. are usually used with such an outfit. The medium weight outfit is best for "all-around" surf fishing since it can also be used for bait fishing on the bottom with 3 or 4 oz. sinkers. It can handle most of the fish found in the surf up to big striped bass and channel bass.

The heavy surf spinning rod will run from about 9 to 12 ft. in over-all length and will have a butt section going from 20 to 28 in. in length. Such heavy rods will handle the heaviest lures made for surf fishing, ranging from 2 to 5 oz. in weight, and sinkers up to 5 or 6 oz. With such a rod you can cast such lures as heavy metal squids, plugs, rigged eels, and large baits used for big striped bass. You can use lines testing anywhere from 20 to 40 lb. The heavy outfit is better than the light or medium outfit for fishing around obstructions, in heavy surf and currents, and for the largest fish. However, the heavy surf spinning outfit, together with a big surf spinning reel, adds up to a lot of weight. It is tiring to use such an outfit for continuous casting or squidding with artificial lures. It is most suitable for sporadic casting with lures or for fishing on the bottom with natural baits. It is also used in certain areas such as Cape Cod, parts of Rhode Island, Montauk, New York, and North Carolina, where heavy lures and baits, long casts, and big fish call for such gear.

A surf spinning rod made from a fast taper blank is the best one to get for all-around fishing. Such rods have fairly light tips, which flex and bend enough to cast the lighter lures or weights, and progressively stiffer and more powerful middle and butt sections, which are brought into play when heavier lures are used. So it is possible to obtain a rod in the medium weight class which will handle a wide variety of lures ranging from 1 to 4 oz. and even a bit heavier if needed. Because of this versatility, there is less need nowadays to buy two or three surf spinning rods. If you buy a medium weight rod which can handle most of the lures and sinkers used in surf fishing, you'll have an outfit suitable for most of your fishing in the surf.

The length of the surf spinning rod will vary according to the manufacturer. The length you use will depend on your fishing area and personal preference. The shorter, lighter rods are best if you do a lot of fishing from jetties, breakwaters, and rocky shores, where you stand high above the water and use mostly artificial lures for small or medium sized fish. But if you fish from beaches where extra long casts and heavy sinkers or baits are used for big fish, you'll find the longer, more powerful rods more suitable. These will not only handle the heavier lures and bigger fish better but also the longer rigs and will help to keep the line above the waves.

The construction of surf spinning rods varies according to the manufacturer and whether the rod is a one-piece blank or a two section job. One-piece glass rods are very strong and have the best action. They are also lighter than two-piece surf spinning rods because they eliminate the heavy reel seat, wood butt, or ferrules found on two-piece rods. The only disadvantage a one-piece rod offers is its extreme length, which makes it difficult to store and transport. You have to carry such rods outside your car and keep them in a basement, garage, or other place that is high and roomy.

The two-piece surf spinning rods are made in two ways. One way is with a detachable butt section and one-piece tip section. Here you still have to worry about length if the tip section runs from 7 to 9 ft. And the reel seat and wood butt usually used for such rods adds extra weight.

The other method used in making a two-piece surf spinning rod is to cut the glass blank either in the middle or down somewhere near the butt and add a ferrule. This makes a shorter rod for transporting when it is taken apart.

When buying a surf spinning rod, make sure that the ferrules, reel seats, and other parts are strong and well-made. The strain of casting heavy lures, sinkers, and baits, and fighting big fish will break or bend weak parts. The reel seats should have screw-threads and rings or bands which hold the reel firmly in place. Sliding rings, which are used on the lighter fresh-water rods, are not secure or dependable for surf fishing.

The guides on a surf spinning rod should be wrapped on securely, and there should be enough of them to distribute the strain of casting and fighting a fish evenly along the rod. Most surf spinning rods are made with graduating guides, with the first and second gathering guides nearest the reel of extra large diameter. When you sight along the rod, these guides should line up perfectly; and you should be able to see through all of them, from the largest to the smallest at the tip. The guides should be of a hard substance which will take the wear of nylon or other synthetic lines. The tip or top guide, especially, should be of a hard material so that grooves aren't worn in the ring. Some anglers still use guides of genuine agate. Although these are extremely hard, they are also brittle; and a sharp rap against a rock will often crack them. The better metal guides today are usually made of tungsten or carboloy.

Many of the salt-water spinning reels covered in the preceding chapter can also be used for surf fishing. It wasn't too long ago that surf anglers had trouble finding reels sturdy enough and big enough for their type of fishing. Now, however, there's a good assortment from which to choose. Surf spinning reels come in different sizes, but generally fall into two classes: the smaller reels which are used with the light and medium outfits, and the larger ones which are used with the heavier surf outfits. The smaller sizes hold anywhere from 200 to 300 yd. of line testing from 10 to 20 lb. The larger reels hold anywhere from 200 to 400 yd. or more of line testing from 15 to 30 lb. When it comes to casting long distances with the heavier lines, large spools are required. So some of the biggest so-called "offshore" spinning reels are also popular with surf anglers using heavy outfits.

Most of the features found in any good salt-water spinning reel, covered in the previous chapter, are also required in a surf spinning reel. It should be made of strong, non-corrosive parts, have a smooth working drag, anti-reverse, dependable bail or pick-up, hard roller, and big handle knob.

The type of line pick-up found on a surf spinning reel is mostly a matter of personal preference. But a full bail automatic pick-up is usually preferred by most surf anglers over a finger or arm pick-up or manual type. The automatic bail pick-up is the most convenient and fastest to use. This is especially desirable if you cast with artificial lures. When the lure hits the water, you can start the retrieve almost immediately with an automatic full bail pick-up. But with a spinning reel having a manual pick-up, there may be a short delay before the line is caught and you can start the retrieve. If a fish strikes when the lure hits the water, you may not be able to set the hook. The delay in starting the retrieve, however short, may cause the lure to sink and foul on the bottom or rocks in shallow water.

Manual pick-ups, however, are almost foolproof and are very dependable. There are fewer parts to go out of order, no bail or finger to bend, and less chance for the line to foul around the bail or arm or finger as often happens on a windy day or when too much slack line develops. So some anglers prefer manual pick-ups. Many reels can be converted from a full bail to a manual pick-up simply by removing the bail. In others you may have to buy an extra part or two to make this conversion.

The roller over which the line runs when retrieved should be of some hard substance in a surf spinning reel. The monofilament lines used will quickly cut grooves in a soft metal roller. The roller should turn freely if it's supposed to do so; and it should be made of very hard metal, sapphire, or agate.

Most spinning reels used in the surf have an anti-reverse lock which, of course, prevents the handle from turning backwards when it is in the "on" position. The majority of surf anglers leave the anti-reverse on while casting and retrieving so that if a fish hits and gets hooked, they are all set. Then if their hand slips off the reel handle or they have to remove their hand to grab a fish or gaff, they have no trouble. If you object to the noise made by a reel with the anti-reverse "on," you can cast with it "off." But you have to get into the habit of flipping the anti-reverse on soon after a fish is hooked.

The handle knob on a surf spinning reel revolves so often when an angler is casting and reeling in lures that there is a lot of wear at this point. Try to get a reel which has a metal bushing to take this wear instead of the plastic knob itself. Otherwise you'll have to replace the plastic knobs on surf spinning reels continually.

The drag on a surf spinning reel should be smooth and constant. A jerky or binding drag will break lines and lose big fish.

Once the drag has been adjusted and set, it should stay that way without changing unless you desire to do so. As a rule, fish hooked in the surf never take too long a run; so the drag, once set, can remain that way throughout the fight. The only time you may have to tighten the drag is when you get the fish in the breakers and the undertow is strong.

When you buy a surf spinning reel, it's a good idea to buy two extra spools. One spool can be filled with the same test line as on the reel just in case you lose a lot of line. The other spool can be filled with a heavier test line in the event you run into some big fish or have to fish in a spot where there are strong currents or obstructions around.

It is important to have the spool on the reel filled properly with the right amount of line. Too much line on the spool will cause it to jump off prematurely and cause line snarls. Too little line on the spool cuts down your casting distance. You can fill the reel spool so that the line comes up to about $\frac{1}{8}$ of an inch from the edge of the lip of the spool. If you find that is a bit too much, you can always cut off a few feet.

Casting with a surf spinning outfit isn't much different in theory or practice than casting with any other spinning outfit, except that you use a two-handed instead of a one-handed rod as in most fresh-water spinning. One common cast generally used with the shorter rods calls for holding the rod in front of you at about the 10 o'clock position just as you do with a fresh-water rod. However, since you use two hands with a surf spinning rod, one hand (the right) will be above the reel, while the other hand will hold the end of the butt.

With a full bail pick-up spinning reel, you turn the handle with your left hand until the line roller is on top. Then you grab the line with the index finger of your right hand, after which you back off the reel handle so that the line is freed from the roller. The last step is to push the wire bail down until it is at the bottom of the reel or out of the way.

Then, with the rod pointing at the target or 10 o'clock position, bring it back quickly over your head. Let it go back to about the 2 o'clock position; and as the lure bends the tip into an arc, start the forward cast by pushing with your right hand and pulling back with your left. As the rod reaches the original position in front of you (10 o'clock), release the line from your right index finger to allow the lure to sail out. When the lure reaches the target, you can stop it by placing your index finger on the lip of the spool or by turning the reel handle forward with your left hand to catch the line and stop it.

Casting with surf spinning rod

Another cast which can be used with a surf spinning rod is similar to the one used with conventional surf rods. Here you simply grab the line in your right index finger and prepare the reel for casting. Then raise the rod to shoulder height and extend it behind you, parallel to the ground. Now, with a quick forward thrust, bring the rod over your head in front of you, releasing the line soon after it passes the vertical position. This cast is best when used with heavy or long surf spinning rods, where the method of casting described above may prove awkward or tiring.

Smooth casting with surf spinning rods will require some practice to achieve the correct timing. The greatest difficulty encountered is the release of the line by the index finger. If this is done too soon, the lure will sail high into the air. If it is done too late, the lure will drop in front of you a short distance away.

Although you have no backlash problems with surf spinning reels, you have to watch for loose coils of line. They may cause line snarls and tangles which may prove difficult to untangle. If such a loose coil or coils develop, try not to reel more line over them. Instead, push the bail down, and back up to allow line to come off the reel spool until you eliminate the loose coils.

All in all, though, a surf spinning outfit is much easier to cast with than a conventional type. Surf spinning tackle has made it possible for the average angler who hasn't much time to practice casting to go out and cast far enough to reach and hook various surf fishes.

13
CONVENTIONAL SURF RODS AND REELS

The conventional surf rod has been used for at least a hundred years by surf fishermen seeking striped bass, channel bass, weakfish, bluefish, and other species. The early surf rods were only about 7 or 8 ft. in over-all length and were made from solid woods such as ash, lancewood, greenheart, and hickory. They were later replaced by cane rods such as the Calcutta and split-bamboo types. The rods were also made longer, with 9 or 9½ ft. rods the most popular. Split-bamboo rods were the favorite right up until a few years after World War II. Then hollow glass surf rods were introduced, and now they have replaced those made from other materials.

The split-bamboo rods did a good job of casting and fighting fish in the surf, but they were undependable. You never knew when the rod would break on a cast or while fighting a fish. The split-bamboo rods also took a permanent "set" or curve from the strain of casting, and they required a lot of care. Surf anglers were always washing their rods in fresh water, drying them, and applying several coats of varnish throughout the fishing season.

When the glass fiber rods made an appearance, they put an end to all this fuss and bother. Today you can use a glass rod without washing or varnishing it except for the wrappings on the guides. Glass rods do not take a permanent set or curve, do not rot, and are not affected by heat, cold, or moisture. They are also extremely strong and light and will last for many years with just ordinary or minimum care. All these qualities make glass rods especially suited to surf fishing, where other rod materials take a beating from casting and using heavy lures, salt water, and the elements in general.

Most beginners starting surf fishing today first buy a spinning surf rod and spinning reel to match. They find it much easier to cast with a spinning surf outfit than with a conventional type. However, the conventional rod and reel has reached a peak of perfection which makes it a very dependable and versatile surf fishing outfit.

Most conventional surf rods fall into one of three divisions: light, medium, and heavy. The light surf rod will run from about 8 to 9½ ft. in over-all length. The tip will be fairly limber to handle lures from about 1 to 2½ oz. and sinkers up to 3 or 4 oz. Such a conventional rod is usually used for relatively calm waters or light surf with few obstructions such as rocks, jetties, and piles. It is mostly used for the smaller fish weighing up to 20 or 30 pounds found in the surf. It can be used for bottom fishing with light sinkers but is not the best rod for this purpose. Such conventional rods in the light class are usually used with lines testing 25 to 30 lb.

The medium weight conventional surf rod is the best one to use for most surf fishing conditions. Such a rod will run from 8½ to 10 ft. in over-all length. It should be limber enough to cast lures as light as 1½ oz. but with enough backbone to handle lures up to 3 or 4 oz. and sinkers up to 5 or 6 oz. If you can afford only one conventional surf rod, this is the weight and action to get. It is the nearest thing to an "all-around" rod for most surf fishing conditions. It will handle most of the lures made for surf fishing yet serve as a good bait stick for surf bottom fishing. Such a rod is usually used with lines testing 36 lb., and it will handle most of the fish found in the surf.

The heavy surf rod is a special tool designed for certain fishing conditions. Such a rod may run anywhere from 9 to 12 ft. in over-all length. The heavy surf rod will handle lures up to 4 or 5 oz. and sinkers up to 6 or 8 oz. It is used mostly to cast these heavy weights long distances and to fight and beach big fish in areas where strong currents, heavy surf, and undertow or obstructions prevail. It is also the best rod to use if you do a lot of bait fishing with heavy sinkers and big chunks of bait. In fact, such a rod, because of its weight, is very tiring for the average person to use any length of time, especially for continuous casting of artificial lures. Yet for those who have the strength and stamina, it is the ideal rod to use in some areas and under certain conditions. You'll find the big, heavy surf rods being used on Cape Cod, parts of Rhode Island, Montauk, New York, North Carolina, and along the Pacific Coast.

Most conventional rods are made in two sections, with a tip and a butt. The butt is detachable at the reel seat, and the rod breaks down into two sections for carrying or transporting. Such a rod can usually be stowed in a car, carried on a train or bus, and can be hidden in a closet. Therefore it is popular with the city dweller who lives in an apartment where long one-piece rods are cumbersome.

The butt sections on such two-piece surf rods run anywhere from 20 to 32 in. in length. When buying a surf rod, get a butt which suits your arm length and feels right when casting. A man with short arms, for example, will feel uncomfortable holding and casting a long butt, while a man with long arms will feel cramped using a short butt. When fishing mostly from sand beaches, you'll find the longer butts better for casting and retrieving lures and baits. When fishing from rocky shores or jetties, you'll find the shorter butts less awkward to use when casting, retrieving, and working lures.

One-piece conventional surf rods are popular with those who live near the beaches and with those surf anglers who have the space for keeping them and cars for transporting the long glass blanks. Rod-carriers are sold for attaching to the side or top of cars, and these make it possible to carry the longest one-piece surf rods. One-piece surf rods are strong, light, and give no trouble at the reel seat or ferrule as two-piece rods often do. The two-piece rods twist or get loose at the ferrule or reel seat, especially after they have been used for a few years.

You can buy one-piece surf rods already made up in most coastal fishing tackle stores. Or you can buy a glass blank, guides, reel seat or clamps, grips and handles, and nylon thread, and make up your own rod. By doing this you can make the rod the exact length and action you want by cutting either from the tip or butt section or both. You can also attach your reel on the rod in the position in which it feels just right for casting.

The early wood and split-bamboo conventional rods were made with one or two guides and a tip-top, but in recent years it was found that several guides did a much better job when casting and in distributing the strain while fighting a fish. So today most well-made conventional surf rods have a minimum of three guides for the short, stiff tips, and as many as six guides and tip-top for the longer, limber rods.

The length of the conventional surf rod you use will depend on your height, weight, and build; where you fish; and the lures, bait, or rigs you cast. A short, lightweight man will have trouble handling some of the heavier, longer rods. And a tall, husky guy will feel uncomfortable and cramped casting with a short, light rod. Using a long rod doesn't automatically guarantee you greater distance when casting. You can cast far enough in the surf to catch fish with short 6 or 7 ft. rods. However, the longer rods are better for "all-around" use in various places and under different conditions. You can use the shorter rods from jetties and rocky shores where you stand above the water level. But if you wade out on a sand bar or rock bar up to your hips, you'll find a short rod a big handicap when it comes to casting and working lures.

A short rod is also out of place when it comes to casting bait rigs, which may have leaders 3 ft. long. Here a long rod makes it easier to handle and cast such clumsy rigs. And if you like to take a long lead from rod tip to lure when casting, you'll find the longer rods permit you to do this. Also, the longer rod will enable you to cast a wider range of lures than a short rod.

But casting is only a small part of surf fishing. You can catch huge striped bass almost at your feet. Actually, 90 per cent of your fish in the surf are hooked within the 200 ft. mark. Almost any surf rod, no matter what length, can reach this distance with ease. More important than casting is where you cast, how you work the lure or bait, and fighting the fish successfully after it is hooked. Under most surf fishing conditions, the longer surf rod is better than the short one. With a longer rod you can give your lure better action by guiding it around obstructions, over breaking waves, and keep it from sinking and fouling on rocky bottoms. You can also do a better job of fighting and handling your fish with the longer rods.

However, it is mostly a matter of personal preference; and you should try various lengths to see which one suits you and your fishing area best. Nowadays you can find almost exactly the length and action of conventional surf rod that you want. If you have trouble along this line, you can always make up your own rod by buying the glass blank and component parts in any coastal fishing tackle store.

The conventional surf reel has come a long way since the first ones were used for striped bass a hundred years ago. The modern conventional revolving spool surf reel is almost foolproof, casts and works smoothly, and is durable. A good reel will last for many years with only an occasional part replacement if it is oiled, cleaned, and taken care of.

Today, conventional surf reels are made with light metal or

plastic spools. Such lightweight spools start to revolve sooner and stop quicker than the heavy metal spools used in the past on most surf reels. This is a big factor in preventing over-runs or backlashes.

Most of the standard surf reels also have wide spools. These are used by many anglers, but the width of such spools often makes it difficult for a person with small hands and fingers to spread the line evenly on the spool. If the line is spooled un-evenly, you have to be extremely careful on the next cast to prevent a backlash. For this reason, many surf anglers prefer the regular or narrow width spools, which make it easier to spool the line more evenly.

A few reels designed for surf fishing come with level-winding devices for spooling the line back on the reel evenly. They work fine although they tend to cut down your casting distance. And if any sand gets into the level-wind mechanism, it can stop it from working. So such reels require more cleaning, oiling, and care not to get sand on them while fishing.

Many surf reels also have anti-backlash devices, which help prevent overruns. These work on different principles such as air brakes or magnets, which control the speed of the revolving spool during the cast. Some of them can be adjusted to match the weight of the lure you are using. Such devices help the beginner a lot, and even expert anglers find them useful when night fishing or when short casts or medium distance casts are required. But most expert surf anglers insist that such anti-backlash devices tend to cut down their casting distance, so they remove them or turn them completely off and depend on their educated thumbs to prevent overruns.

The star drag found on most conventional surf reels is important since it helps when fighting a big fish and takes the shock of the initial strike. The drag, of course, acts as a brake and can be adjusted to suit the strength of the line and the size of the fish. You turn the star forward or backward to increase or

Garcia salt-water Mitchell No. 302 is popular for surf fishing. It holds 300 yd. of 20 lb. test Platyl mono line.

Luxor No. 3 Mer salt-water spinning reel is used by surf anglers for heavy fishing. It holds 250 yd. of 25 lb. test mono line.

The Alcedo Mark IV salt-water spinning reel is one of the largest made for surf fishing. It holds 700 yd. of 14 lb. test mono line.

Langley Dyna-matic Model 444 can be shifted from free-spool to either 3 to 1 or 6 to 1 gear ratio. It has a one-piece body construction.

Harnell conventional surf rod has a 7 ft. tip and 30 in. detachable butt. It is listed as a medium weight squidding rod.

Harnell Ultimate surf casting and squidding rods come in 9 and 10 ft. lengths and light and heavy actions.

Pfleuger Sea King is a surf reel with extra wide spool, take-apart, and free-spool push button. It holds 320 yd. of 27 lb. test line.

Ocean City Inductor has powerful permanent magnets in sideplate which help prevent backlash. It holds 200 yd. of 9-thread line.

Penn Leveline reel has a spiral bar which helps spread the line evenly on the spool. It holds 200 yd. of 27 lb. test ine.

This Harnell glass rod for offshore fishing is made in light and medium weights. It has a 5 ft. 6 in. tip, six or seven guides, and a roller tip-top.

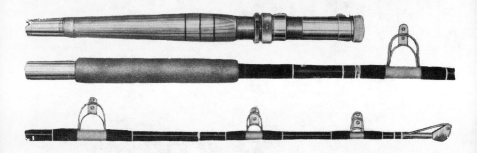

Harnell big-game rods come in heavy and extra heavy actions for the largest fish. They have roller guides, lock-top reel seat, and cork foregrips.

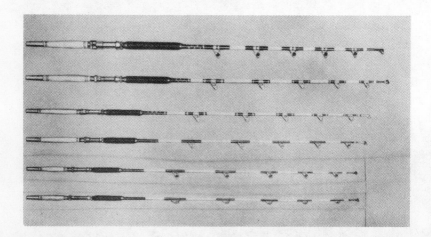

Tycoon/Fin-Nor glass rods are available for all kinds of offshore fishing with a choice for various test lines from 12 to 130 lb.

The Penn Master Mariner reel is popular for light offshore trolling and can be used with linen, synthetic, and wire lines. It is made in four models with a choice of gear ratios and a convertible star drag.

Ocean City Big Game reels come in sizes from 4/0 to 16/0 and feature cup type drag assembly which can be removed without disassembling side plate of reel.

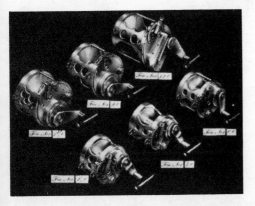

Fin-Nor big-game reels come in the different sizes shown for all classes of offshore fishing. They are expensive but are noted for their smooth performance and durability.

Pfleuger Ohio reel comes in two sizes and is often used for salt-water bottom fishing.

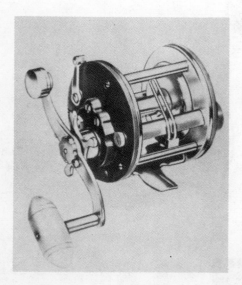

Penn Monofil reel is popular for all kinds of bottom fishing with mono-filament and other lines. It features a level-wind, free-spool, and star-drag.

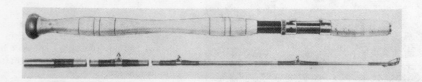

Wright & McGill Trollrod is used for trolling and bottom fishing from boats, banks, and piers. It comes in four lengths from 6 to 7½ ft.

Pfleuger Medalist in the largest size is a popular salt-water fly fishing reel.

Below. Garcia Ambassadeur reels are popular with salt-water popping anglers and bait casters. These reels have a level-wind, free-spool, and star drag.

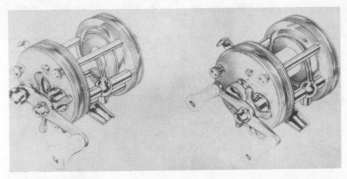

Fin-Nor fly reels come in different sizes for all kinds of salt-water fly fishing. They have the quick adjusting drag for light to heavy braking while the fish is being fought.

Harnell Ultimate live bait and boat rods come in various lengths from 8 to 15 ft. and in light and heavy actions.

Harnell black glass fly rod comes in 9½ ft. length. It is available with or without detachable belly butt. This rod is recommended for salmon, steelhead, and salt-water fly fishing.

Shakespeare Co. heavy duty bait-casting rod for musky fishing also makes a good rod for salt-water bait-casting.

decrease the braking action. The drag should work smoothly on the reel you buy, and most modern reels are dependable in this respect. However, after using the reel for long periods, the drag washers may wear or may become soaked with oil. Then the worn ones should be replaced, and the oil-soaked washers should be cleaned and dried.

Conventional surf reels have a higher gear ratio than the salt-water reels used for bottom fishing or offshore fishing. A gear ratio of at least three to one is a must on surf reels if you use artificial lures. With such a reel the spool turns three times for every turn of the handle. This permits you to retrieve artificial lures faster and also to take up slack line more quickly.

The Langley Corporation makes a reel called the Dynamatic 444, which has a two-speed retrieve. With the flip of a lever you can retrieve your lure or bait either at three to one or a six to one gear ratio rate. This enables a surf angler to retrieve his lure at a fast speed at the six to one ratio. But when he hooks a fish, he can change to the three to one ratio to play and land it. The gears of this reel are meshed automatically before engagement to eliminate the possibility of stripping them. Such a fast retrieve on a surf reel is a great aid when reeling sinking lures over shallow rocky bottoms. The fast speed enables you to keep the lure riding high at all times, and it also enables the surf angler to give his lure better action when it is caught by an incoming wave. Also, some fish will strike a fast moving lure when they'll pass up a slower moving one.

Many surf reels also have a "take-apart" feature consisting of a screw which, when released, enables you to take out the spool and reach some of the working parts of the reel. This permits quick changing of spools and cleaning and oiling of the reel.

Surf reels come in different sizes, holding anywhere from 150 to 250 yd. of 27 or 36 lb. test line. The smaller reels holding about 150 yd. of line are used with the lighter outfits. The 200 yd. size can be used with the medium or "all-around" surf fishing outfit. The larger 250 yd. reels can be used with the heavier surf outfits where extra line or larger sized lines such as the 45 or 50 lb. test are used.

Most of the companies such as Penn, Pflueger, and True Temper or Ocean City which make surf fishing reels today have been doing so for many years and offer dependable products and services. Surf reels range from $10.00 to $30.00 in price.

Before casting with a conventional outfit, you must make sure that you have the proper amount of line on the reel. The line should be spooled on the reel under a light tension so that it packs down evenly and compactly. This can be done by having another person hold the spool of line between both hands and applying some pressure against the sides of the spool. If you do it alone, hold the line between two fingers of your left hand and squeeze as you reel it on. When the line reaches a point about 1/4 of an inch from the bar supports on the reel, you have enough line on the spool. Too much line may rub against these bars, while too little makes casting more difficult and cuts down your distance.

After the reel is filled with line, attach it to the rod; and you are ready to cast. The best place to cast is into a body of water where the line will get wet. And in the beginning, use a heavy lure or sinker weighing at least 3 or 4 oz.

To cast, stand with legs well apart. Assuming you are at a beach, your body is at a right angle to the ocean and faces down the beach along the water line. Next, throw the reel into free-spool and let out about 3 ft. of line. In other words, the lure or weight hangs so that it's about 3 ft. from the tip of the rod. Hold the butt of the rod with your right hand under the reel. Your left hand holds the end of the butt. Your thumb presses against the line or reel spool. Raise the rod so that it's almost shoulder high.

Now, with a quick forward thrust, bring your rod tip over

Surf casting with conventional rod and reel

your head. As you push forward with your right hand, pull back with your left hand. Your body twists toward the target; and when your rod tip passes the vertical position, remove your thumb from the reel spool. But put it back quickly to feel the line running out under your thumb. As it moves out, apply pressure, depending on the speed of the spool. If it's going too fast, press down a bit; if too slow, ease off with your thumb. When the weight or lure reaches the target, stop the cast with your thumb.

It takes many hours of practice until you get the correct timing and feel of the proper thumbing to apply during a cast. In the beginning don't try for distance, but be satisfied with short casts. Practice spooling the line on the reel evenly at all times. This alone will help prevent many backlashes. If you find that the line is uneven on the reel spool, take it easy on the next cast.

14

OFFSHORE RODS AND REELS

When the first pioneer big-game anglers set out in small boats to hook and fight the "monsters of the deep," they used fishing rods and reels which were pitifully inadequate. The rods were light models similar to those used at the time for striped bass, channel bass, and tarpon. They were made from such woods as blackpalm, greenheart, lancewood, snakewood, hickory, and split-bamboo. The reels were also small and held only 250 or 300 yd. of 21-thread line. They had no drags and instead depended on a leather pad, which the angler pressed with his thumb to apply tension.

With such tackle, Dr. Charles F. Holder landed a tuna weighing 183 lb. in 1898 off Santa Catalina Island, California. Shortly afterwards he helped organize the Catalina Tuna Club there, and members set tackle regulations which limited the rod tip to 16 oz. and the line to 24-thread. Then members of this club went on to make many light tackle catches of tuna, marlin, and swordfish.

However, in the years following, big-game tackle was greatly improved; and it was discovered that heavier tackle was needed to battle and boat such fish as giant tuna, the larger marlin, swordfish, and sharks. Such fish sometimes reach 1000 lb. and more, and the lighter tackle used off California in the early days was not heavy enough to subdue the biggest ones. So big-game tackle went to an extreme; and big, heavy rods weighing up to 50 oz, 20/0 reels, and 72-thread lines were used during the 1930's. Actually such heavy tackle never became too popular with the average offshore fisherman. It was too expensive, required a husky man to handle it effectively, and most of the time was used for fish which were too light to put it to a real test. Big fish near or over the 1000 lb. mark are not too common. Most offshore fish caught range between the 30 and 500 lb. class. This includes most of the sailfish, marlins, tuna, and swordfish. In certain areas and during certain seasons, of course, many fish may be caught over the 500 lb. mark; for example, swordfish and black marlin off Peru or Chile or the giant tuna off Nova Scotia. However, the fact remains that the great majority of offshore fish fall below the 500 lb. mark. Many offshore fishermen have to settle for the smaller bluefish, bonito, albacore, dolphin, barracuda, amberjack, wahoo, or king mackerel, which are generally less than 100 lb. in weight.

Big-game anglers soon discovered that they were using tackle too heavy and too strong for the fish they were catching. During the past twenty years or so, offshore tackle has been getting lighter and lighter. The new glass rods, dependable reels with smooth drags, and uniform synthetic lines have done much to bring this about. Now an offshore angler can venture out on the deep water with more confidence that his tackle will stand up.

The original offshore rods made from solid woods were never very good. Hickory rods were popular for the biggest fish such as giant tuna for a time. But they had to be made from the best grade of wood and even then were apt to break or take a bad set. Split-bamboo rods enjoyed quite a vogue for many years in offshore fishing. So did the various laminated rods. which were made from strips of wood in vertical, horizontal, or horizontal-vertical combinations. Such rods are still being made and used in offshore fishing, but the trend has been more and more toward glass rods.

Today you can find a glass rod for almost any kind of offshore fishing you plan to do, from the lightest to the heaviest. The excellent properties of Fiberglas are too well known to repeat here. These same qualities make glass rods the best ones yet developed for offshore fishing. Most of the rods are made from hollow glass blanks; but solid glass blanks are also used, especially for the less expensive offshore rods.

Most offshore rods have a tip section of 5 or 5½ ft. and butts ranging from 15 to 21 in. The best butts are usually made from second growth straight grained hickory. The cheaper rods may have butts made from ash.

The reel seat on an offshore rod should be of the screw-locking type which holds the rod tip firmly aligned and the reel tightly in place. The double locking ring type reel seats are best and hold the reel securely in place under all conditions. The reel seat should be well made, sturdy, and heavily chrome-plated.

The regular ringed metal guides are used on the lighter offshore rods; but for the heavier models, roller guides are preferred. Even on the cheaper and lighter rods, a roller tip-top is generally used. The roller guides are usually made of metal with stainless steel rollers. Some have anodized aluminum frames, while other guides are made from nylon frames and feet. The nylon type roller guides flex with the rod and do not stiffen the action in any way. Of course, the roller is still of stainless steel, even in the nylon or light metal guides. The rollers should run freely and should be cleaned and oiled occasionally. The roller guides can usually be disassembled by removing a screw.

Offshore rods fall into various classifications based on official specifications set up by different fishing clubs and the International Game Fish Association. When all rods were made from wood, the weights of the rod tips were used to designate the different tackle specifications and divisions. Likewise, when linen lines were used for offshore fishing, the line was rated according to the number of threads. Thus balanced offshore outfits were called 4/6, 6/9, and so on up to 36/54. The first number stood for the weights of the rod tip, and the second one indicated the line thread to be used. So a 6/9 outfit meant that the rod tip would weigh no more than 6 oz., and it was to be used with 9-thread line.

When glass rods and synthetic lines appeared, however, it was necessary to make changes. Glass rods are either hollow or solid and come in different wall thicknesses, so there are great variations in weight. Braided synthetic lines are rated according to the pound test instead of threads, so this also required a new system. The International Game Fish Association decided that fish records and tackle classifications should be based on the line size or test. They established separate divisions for 12, 20, 30, 50, 80, 130 and 180 lb. test lines.

So now rod manufacturers making offshore rods design them in weights and actions for use with the various strength lines. The flexibility of the rod is judged by the deflection method. A specified weight anywhere from 1 to 10 lb. is used, depending on the line test. A rod is supposed to deflect or bend a certain number of inches for a specific classification. For most practical purposes, however, you can choose a rod designed for a certain strength line and be pretty certain that it will perform well with that pound test.

To simplify matters, we can divide the offshore rods into four classes: light, medium, heavy, and extra-heavy. The light rods are used with lines testing 12 to 30 lb. or with 3, 6 or 9-thread linen lines and will have a flexible action to handle such light lines. The light outfit is ideal to use for the smaller offshore fish such as bluefish, bonito, albacore, dolphin, barracuda, king mackerel, and similar fish weighing from about 5 to 50 lb.

The medium weight offshore rods are used with lines testing from 30 to 70 lb. or with the 12, 15, 18 and 21-thread linen lines. Such rods are used for sailfish, white marlin, striped marlin, school tuna, amberjack, and similar fish ranging from 50 to 300 lb.

The heavy offshore rods are used with lines testing from 70 to 130 lb. or with the 24, 36 and 39-thread linen lines. Such rods are best for the bigger fish such as blue marlin, swordfish, giant tuna, and sharks, or in other words, when you expect to catch fish ranging from about 300 to 1000 lb.

Then we have the extra-heavy offshore rods, used with lines testing from 130 to 180 lb. Such heavy rods and lines are used to tackle the real deep-sea monsters such as the largest swordfish, blue marlin, black marlin, giant tuna, and sharks as well as any other fish in the 1000 lb. class and up.

Naturally, you don't have to follow official club or IGFA specifications if you're not interested in records. You can use any combinations of rod, reel, or line you like, according to your own ideas. Beginners or casual anglers can use somewhat heavier tackle until they become more experienced, while experts can go as light as they want for the maximum in sport and fun.

Offshore fishing reels have also come a long way since the days when the Catalina Tuna Club anglers tackled the big fish in the Pacific Ocean. The first reels used in salt-water fishing not only lacked star-drags but also free-spools. When a big fish took hold and started to run, the reel handles would be a whirling blur and extremely dangerous. Many an early big-game angler suffered injuries when the fast revolving reel handles struck his hand. Such early "knuckle-busting" reels prevented the pioneer offshore anglers from tackling the biggest gamefish in the sea.

It wasn't until 1911, when William C. Boschen perfected the star-drag reel, that anglers really got a practical salt-water reel for big-game fishing. Boschen, who was an ardent angler, went out in 1913 and landed a world's record swordfish, which weighed 355 lb., using his reel off Catalina Island. Boschen refused to commercialize his hobby of big-game fishing by taking a patent on the star-drag reel. He also wanted as many anglers as possible to have the opportunity of using his latest development. Therefore he turned it over to Julius Vom Hofe of Brooklyn, who made and marketed these big-game reels with star-drags. From then on anglers started going after bigger and bigger ocean fish as the reels increased in size and efficiency.

The star-drag on the big-game reels consists, of course, of a series of alternating leather and metal washers which can be tightened to various tensions to exert a drag on the reel spool which prevents a fish from taking line too readily. The fish must pull against this tension and therefore can't take line too fast or too easily. Naturally this helps to tire a big fish much sooner.

Most star-drag reels have a "star" wheel which is located under the handle; and this is turned forward to tighten the drag and back to loosen it. However, one reel, the Fin-Nor, makes use of a lever which is pushed forward or back to adjust the drag tension. There is a half-circle track with holes under the lever, and you can fit a spring stop on the lever into any particular hole to get tthe desired drag tension.

Instead of leather washers in the drag assembly, some modern reels like the Penn Senator make use of asbestos automobile brake lining for the drag material. These wear longer and exert a more powerful, smoother brake action.

All big-game reels have a free-spool mechanism, which is turned on or off with a lever. This permits the reel spool to revolve freely without turning the gears or handle. It is used to let out line or drop a bait back to a fish and in other fishing operations. Once the fish it hooked, of course, the free spool is not used because the drag takes over.

As a reel increases in size, the gear ratio between the handle and spool decreases. A high gear ratio of three to one or higher is needed in a surf casting or other small reel because the diameter of the spool is small, and the high gear ratio enables you to reel in line faster. But the big-game reels have large diameter spools, and line is retrieved fast enough for all practical purposes. Besides, a high gear ration places a strain on the gears themselves, with the danger of stripping. So most of the largest big-game sized reels have a gear ratio of two to one or less, although the smaller sized offshore reels may still be four to one or three to one.

The spools on big-game reels must be large and strong. They are subjected to terrific strains when fighting and pumping big fish, especially when used with synthetic lines, which compress and expand against the spool flanges. Weak spools will buckle or break under the strain, so most of the modern big-game reels have solid one-piece cast or forged metal spools of extra strength.

Some big-game reels are made to be attached to the rod with clamps, wing-nuts, or rod braces. Most of the larger reels also have lugs or eyelets on top of the frames for attaching to the snaps on harnesses. The handles are usually long and have thick knobs large enough to be gripped firmly with the hand.

Reels for offshore fishing are designated by the numbers 1/0, 2/0, 3/0, 4/0 and so on up to 20/0, which the largest. However, for most practical big-game fishing, the 16/0 is about the largest used. These numbers give only a rough indication of the size because each reel manufacturer makes the reel according to his own ideas and specifications. So you'll find a variation in the size even though the number may be the same. A 12/0 reel made by one company may be larger or smaller than a 12/0 by another company. However, they all put out catalogs showing how much line of a certain pound test their reels will hold. This will vary according to the line used since linen, nylon, and dacron have different diameters.

If you plan to do mostly light tackle fishing, the reels No. 1/0, 2/0, 3/0, and 4/0 are best. For medium tackle fishing, the No. 6/0 and 9/0 reels can be used. For heavy tackle, the No. 10/0, and 12/0 and 14/0 reels are the sizes. And for extra-heavy tackle, the 16/0 reel may be needed.

The major big-game reel manufacturers in this country are the Tycoon/Fin-Nor Corp.; the Penn Fishing Tackle Co.; and the True Temper American Tackle Division, which makes the Ocean City big-game reels. The Penn and Ocean City big-game reels are moderately priced, ranging from $20.00 to $150. The Fin-Nor big-game reels are higher priced, ranging from $250 to $645.

15

BOTTOM FISHING RODS, REELS AND RIGS

Bottom fishing is as popular in salt water as still fishing or pan-fishing is in fresh water. It's the sport of the common man who doesn't give a hoot about how he catches fish or exactly what fish he gets just so long as he catches something. But there are many occasions when even the salt-water expert or specialist turns to bottom fishing. This happens when the more glamorous fishes such as striped bass, weakfish, tarpon, snook, sailfish, tuna, or marlin are not around or play hard to get. At such times, the lowly bottom fishes not only provide some sport, fun, and food but also bolster an angler's ego. At least he doesn't go home skunked.

Bottom fishing is done from shore, surf, piers, bridges, rowboats, private craft, and party boats. The fish caught in different parts of the country vary in feeding habits, type of waters in which they are found, and also in size. Methods and techniques of bottom fishing also vary according to the kind of fish, bait used, and the area being fished. To meet these different conditions, bottom fishing tackle is also varied; and no single rod or reel will be able to handle all the situations that arise.

It wasn't too long ago that many bottom fishermen used handlines to catch their fish. Less than fifty years ago you'd see thousands of anglers fishing from bridges, piers, shore, and

141

party boats with heavy cord lines wound around a wooden frame. Such handlines were inexpensive, of course, and often caught fish. But they provided little sport compared to the pleasure obtained from fighting a fish on a limber, yielding rod and light line. And many of the more wary bottom fishes stayed away from the heavy, visible lines and were rarely caught. A few bottom fishermen still use handlines today, but they are rapidly vanishing from the salt-water scene.

Even when bottom fishermen turned to using fishing rods, they demanded, and got, stiff, heavy clubs, which were only a slight improvement over handlines insofar as sport was concerned. These early rods made of solid woods were eventually replaced by split-bamboo rods. While split-bamboo rods are still being used, they are giving way to glass rods, which are not only lighter and more flexible, thus providing more sport and fun, but also are stronger than any of the wooden rods used in the past. Nowadays you'll find bottom fishermen using almost every type of rod made for salt-water fishing, from the lightest to the heaviest.

The rods generally used for bottom fishing are the bay, pier, and boat rods of varying lengths and weights. They run from 5 to 7 ft. in over-all length, and most of them are made of hollow or solid glass. The hollow or tubular rods are lighter than solid glass, but the latter are somewhat cheaper and extremely strong.

The lightest bottom fishing rods are used in protected and shallow water such as bays, sounds, rivers, and inlets for small or medium sized fish. Here you'll find the short bay rods, weakfish, and flounder rods running up to 5 to 6 ft. in over-all length. These rods have light limber tips but fairly heavy wood butts and reel seats. They can usually handle sinkers weighing from 2 to 6 oz. and fish running up to 8 or 10 lb. You'll find these rods being used from shore, piers, bridges, and rowboats for such smaller species as flounders, weakfish, porgies, sea bass, croakers, snappers, and grunts.

In recent years, however, more and more bottom fishermen going after the smaller species in shallow water have been using spinning tackle. Salt-water spinning outfits in the light and medium weight classes are now widely used for bottom fishing in bays and from bridges and piers for such fish. As long as they don't have to handle sinkers over 4 or 5 oz., spinning outfits can be used for this fishing.

Most of the rods used in bottom fishing fall into the medium weight division. These are the popular "boat rods," which are made in two sections with a ferrule in the center or with a one-piece tip section and a detachable butt. They are usually about 5 to 7 ft. in over-all length and have a fairly stiff tip section. This is the rod you usually see on the party boats sailing from Atlantic coast ports. But it is also used from bridges, jetties, shore, and piers. Such a rod will handle the medium sized bottom fish running from 5 to 30 lb. or so. This rod can also be used in deep water and strong currents, which may require sinkers weighing up to 10 or 12 oz.

Quite a few bottom fishermen also like to use the regular conventional and spinning type surf rods from bridges, piers, shore, and party boats. They prefer the longer tips and butts for clearing the pier or boat rails, for handling long rigs, and for casting.

The heaviest bottom fishing outfits are used in areas where the water is extremely deep and heavy sinkers may be required. They are also needed when going after big fish on the bottom. Such rods may have tip sections weighing up to 12 or 14 oz. and big reels holding at least 250 or 300 yd. of line. The lines used may run anywhere from 40 to 80 lb. in strength. Such outfits may be used for big halibut, big groupers, jewfish, the smaller sharks, and rays. Halibut and jewfish may run several hundred pounds in weight, and only the heaviest bottom tackle will be able to hold and land them. If the fishing is done in deep waters, you may need a pound or more of lead to reach and hold bottom.

Bottom fishing reels naturally will match the rod and line you are using. For the light rods and lines and small fish, for example, you would use the smaller reels. Sometimes called bay or pier reels, and they usually hold about 100 or 150 yd. of 15 to 30 lb. test line. Most of them have free-spool and star-drag, and some are made with a level-wind mechanism.

For the medium weight bottom fishing outfits, the "boat" or "light trolling" salt-water reels are mostly used. These usually hold anywhere from 150 to 250 yds. of 30 or 40 lb. test line. These reels also have star-drags, free-spool levers, and come with plastic or metal spools. The plastic spools are best if any casting is being done or when linen, braided nylon, or dacron lines are used. The metal spools are best for monofilament lines to resist the pressure developed when such lines are retrieved under tension. Such pressure exerts itself against the spool flanges and will often break plastic spools. Reel manufacturers now make special reels for fishing with monofilament line. They have extra strong metal spools and are also precision fitted so that the thin mono lines can't get behind the spool and cause trouble.

Anglers who do a lot of bottom fishing from shore, surf, piers, jetties, or boat where casting is required also use surf casting conventional and spinning reels. However, unless very long casts are required, most bottom fishing reels will also cast a sinker and bait a good distance.

For heavy bottom fishing, the largest sized salt-water reels designed for bottom fishing can be used. These may be boat or light trolling reels with capacities of 250 or 300 yd. of 40 to 80 lb. test line. Very few true bottom fishing reels hold so much line; therefore many anglers use the so-called "big-game" or "trolling" reels in the smaller sizes such as 3/0 and 4/0 for heavy bottom fishing.

The rigs used for bottom fishing are very important since they present the bait to the fish at the right level and in the most attractive manner. There are now many "ready-made" rigs which can be used for bottom fishing for sale in most coastal fishing tackle stores. These are called by various names according to the fish they are used for such as flounder rig, fluke rig, codfish rig, etc. Others are simply called deep-sea rigs or bottom rigs, indicating where or how they are used.

Most of these ready-made bottom rigs are very convenient to use and come packaged in transparent envelopes. You can buy a half-dozen and just have to add the hook and sinker. Some of the rigs even have the hooks attached, in which case only the sinker is required. Such rigs often have spreaders or free swinging hook holders which keep the hook and leader away from the main line leading to the sinker. They also have special sinker snaps or holders, permitting the quick attachment and changing of sinkers.

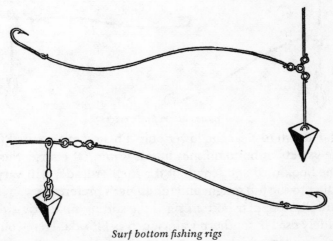

Surf bottom fishing rigs

Although the ready-made rigs are not too expensive and are convenient to buy and use, many bottom fishemen prefer to make up their own rigs. This can easily be done by buying a coil or spool of monofilament line or leader material, hooks, swivels, and sinkers. In Chapter 22 you will find information on tying knots and the different snaps and swivels which can be used for making rigs. Chapter 21 shows and describes the different sinkers which can be used for bottom fishing.

The most commonly used rig in salt water is the basic bottom fishing rig, which is used with one or two hooks. Here you simply tie a three-way swivel a few inches above the sinker and attach a hook on a snell or leader for a one-hook rig. To make a two-hook rig, you attach a second hook above the first one

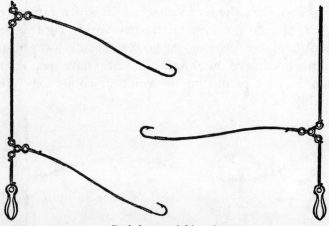

Basic bottom fishing rigs

high enough to clear the lower one. This rig can be used for a wide variety of bottom fishes in salt water. Of course, the size of the hook used and length of the snell or leader will vary according to the fish sought and the angler's preference.

Another popular bottom rig is the sliding sinker rig, which is widely used in southern waters such as Florida. Here you use an egg sinker, which has a hole running through the center.

This sinker is slipped on the fishing line. Then a barrel swivel is tied to the end of the line to act as a stop, after which you attach the leader holding the hook. A variation of this rig is to use a snap-swivel on the line and attach a bank sinker to the

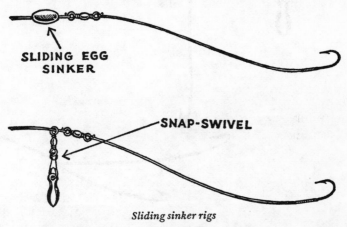

SLIDING EGG
SINKER

SNAP-SWIVEL

Sliding sinker rigs

snap. The fishing line runs through one of the eyes on this snap-swivel. Then another barrel swivel is tied to the end of the fishing line to act as a stop. Then the leader and hook is attached to this barrel swivel. The main idea with sliding sinker rigs is to permit a fish to take line without feeling the weight of the sinker.

To catch flounders, two types of rigs are commonly used. The first is the standard old-time wire spreader flounder rig. This has a wire spreader which separates the two hooks attached to each end. The sinker is attached in the middle. You can buy these spreaders in most fishing tackle stores. If you want a flounder rig with less hardware, you can use the second type. Here the hook is attached a couple of inches or so above the sinker. Then a second hook is tied into the leader of the first one to make a two-hook flounder rig.

The flounder rigs above are used mostly for the smaller winter flounders. For fluke or summer flounders you use the

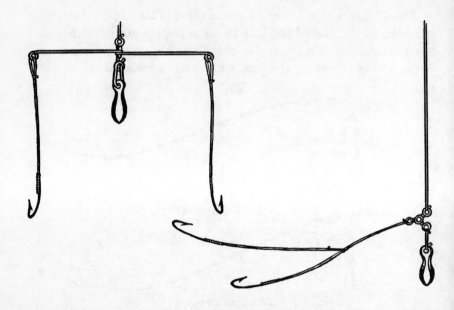

Flounder rigs

fluke rig. Here you have a leader and a hook anywhere from 2 to 3 ft. long. This is tied about 6 in. above the sinker. You can use a single long-shanked plain hook or a double tandem hook to hold the bait. Other anglers attach a two-bladed fluke spinner above the hook.

The high leader rig is good for weakfish, striped bass, and other fish which often swim off the bottom. Here you use a long leader with a hook going anywhere from 3 to 4 ft. This is attached to the main fishing line the same distance (3 or 4 ft.) above the sinker.

If you plan to do any bottom fishing in the surf, you can use two types of rigs. One is the standard surf rig, which makes use of a three-way swivel. The swivel is tied a few inches above a pyramid sinker. The hook and leader is tied to one eye of the

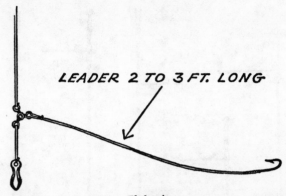

Fluke rig

three-way swivel, and the line is attached to the remaining eye. The other rig is known as the fish-finder. Here you use a fish-finder gadget, which is nothing more than a heavy wire formed with a ring on one end and a snap on the other. If you can't obtain these fish finders, you can use a large sized snap-swivel as a substitute. The ring of the fish-finder device is slipped over the main fishing line. Then a barrel swivel is attached to the

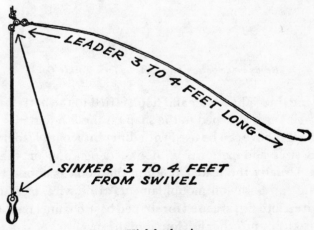

High leader rig

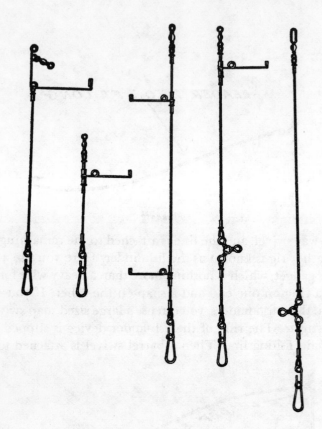

Ready-made bottom rigs made by Jeros Tackle Co.

end of the line. The leader and hook is tied to the barrel swivel while a sinker is attached to the snap on the fish-finder.

Both rigs above can be used with different length leaders and various sizes and patterns of hooks, depending on the fish sought. Usually the leader holding the hook is about 18 in. long and can be nylon monofilament, cable wire, or stainless steel wire. Both rigs are used for striped bass, channel bass, bluefish, weakfish, and other fish found in the surf.

16
OTHER SALT-WATER TACKLE

In addition to the salt-water fishing tackle covered in the previous chapters, there are many other kinds which are used from time to time and for specific fishing. Salt-water anglers also use long cane or glass poles to fish from small boats, shore, piers, bridges, and jetties. These can be anywhere from 10 to 20 ft. long and fairly strong if used for good-sized fish. The lighter, shorter poles are very popular with "snapper" fishermen in North Atlantic coastal waters. These are the small bluefish, which run up to a pound or so but are generally smaller. A piece of monofilament line testing anywhere from 10 to 20 lb. is tied to the end of the cane or glass pole, and a small long-shanked hook is baited with a small, live killie or dead spearing or shiner. A float can be used with this rig if you want to keep the bait a few feet below the surface. Cane poles are also used for any other small fish which comes close to shore such as silver hake or whiting, blackfish or tautog, croakers, spot, sheepshead, snappers, and grunts.

For inshore trolling for such fish as big bluefish, striped bass, channel bass, tarpon, and fish of a similar weight, a trolling rod is used. Such rods usually have tips from 5 to 6 ft. long and weigh anywhere from 8 to 12 oz. The butts range from 14 to 21 in. in length. They can have regular ringed stainless steel guides; but if wire lines are used, they should have Carboloy guides and agate or roller guide tip-tops.

Such inshore trolling outfits are generally used for fish running from 10 to 60 lb.; and braided nylon, dacron, or monofilament lines testing from 36 to 50 lb. are loaded on 3/0 or 4/0 reels.

When casting inshore from a boat for such fish as big striped bass, channel bass, and big bluefish, a rod similar to the conventional surf rod is often used. However, the tip will usually be shorter, going only about 6 to 6½ ft. and the butt will run from 18 to 24 in. but not much longer. Such a rod will have a light or medium surf rod action similar to the "squidding" rods used along the beaches and from jetties. But it should have enough backbone to cast lures up to 3 or 4 oz. and handle the occasional big stripper or channel bass going over 50 lb. Such rods are used with 27, 30, or 36 lb. test braided nylon or dacron lines. The regular conventional surf fishing reels holding 150 or 200 yd. of line work fine with such casting rods.

Another special type of salt-water rod is the so-called "live bait" rod used on the West Coast from the live-bait boats fishing for albacore or yellowtail. These rods are usually long, sometimes up to 12 ft. in over-all length, with light, limber tips for casting the delicate sardines and anchovies used for bait. Such rods are either the conventional type for use with revolving spool reels or the spinning type for use with salt-water spinning reels. The conventional rods have smaller guides while the spinning live-bait rods have the larger type guides. Some of the Harnell rods of this type go up to 15 ft. in length, but this makes them somewhat cumbersome for use on a crowded party boat. Usually a rod of this type from 9 to 12 ft. in over-all length will serve for live-bait fishing. Such rods are used with lines testing anywhere from 10 to 40 lb., depending on the stiffness and action of the blank used. The conventional type rods naturally use heavier lines than most spinning types. Some of the live-bait rods are made for jig casting and can handle lures up to 6 oz. Although boat fishing calls for shorter butts, some companies also make live-bait rods with longer butts to use for surf fishing.

Somewhat similar to the live-bait boat rods on a smaller, shorter scale are the salmon and steelhead mooching rods used in the Pacific Northwest. They usually run from 8 to 10 ft. in over-all length, and the steelhead rods are usually shorter and lighter than those preferred for salmon, especially for the big chinook or king salmon. These rods also come in conventional types or spinning types for use with either reel. They are usually made with light cork handles and grips, have locking reel seats, and are used with monofilament lines testing from 10 to 25 lb.

Then we have the so-called "popping" rods, which are very popular in Florida and the Gulf of Mexico. They became popular years ago in Texas and other Gulf states for fishing in shallow waters for such fish as sea trout, redfish, snook, and small tarpon. In Florida waters they are used for these same fish and other species in the same weight class.

The true popping rod is usually from 6 to 7½ ft. in over-all length. It has a cork handle anywhere from 8 to 17 in. long and a foregrip of 3 or 4 in. The shorter-handled rods are cast with one hand while the longer ones are cast with two hands. Many of these rods also have a finger hook or trigger which is held by the index finger of the right hand while casting. Popping rods usually come in one piece but may be in two sections. The two-piece rods generally have a detachable handle or butt at the reel seat.

Since most of these rods are used with revolving spool reels, they have small guides and screw-locking reel seats for mounting the reel above the rod. Many of the regular bait-casting reels used for fresh-water fishing can be used with these rods. However, since these have smaller spools and are often made of

metals which can't take salt-water, a heavier type casting reel
made for such fishing is preferred. It can be any light, salt-water
casting reel which holds 100 to 150 yd. of 15 or 20 lb. test line.
If the reel has no level-wind attachment, you have to spool the
reel evenly with your left hand when you retrieve it. Much
more convenient is a reel which has a level-wind, free-spool,
and star-drag. There are several such heavy-duty fresh-water
and small salt-water reels on the market.

Salt-water anglers also use bait-casting type rods when casting various lures for small and medium sized fish up to 50 lb.
or so. Some anglers even tackle husky tarpon in the 100 lb. class
on such gear, but this is mostly for the experts. You can use
almost any bait-casting rods made for fresh-water fishing in
salt water, too. But because of the heavier lures used and strain
on the rod from reeling and from fighting fish and tides, a somewhat heavier rod is called for. Most rod manufacturers make
what they call a heavy-duty fresh-water or "musky" bait-casting
rod, and these are also suitable for salt-water use. They range
from 5 to 7 ft. in over-all length and have handles from 8 to 10
in. long. They usually have a finger hook, too. You can buy
them with detachable handles and one-piece tips or in two
sections with a ferrule in the center.

Some of the bait-casting reels made for fresh water can be
used with the bait-casting rods above. But they should be sturdy
and constructed of non-corrosive metals. There are also many
special heavy-duty fresh-water and light salt-water casting reels
with level-winds, free-spool, and star-drag which can be used
with the bait-casting rods for salt water.

Finally, we have the fly rods and reels, which are used in salt-
water for different species. Here again, many anglers use the
same fly rods they use in fresh water and often find that they
serve the purpose. As a general rule, however, the fresh-water
fly rod, unless it is made for heavy fishing, is too light for salt-
water fly fishing. Because of the long casts with big, bulky lures

required and the need for casting into strong winds, the longer, more powerful fly rods do a better job. They help keep the backcast high and also make it easier to manipulate the different fly lures at a distance.

Most expert salt-water fly casters prefer fly rods in the 9 or 9½ ft. lengths for this fishing. Of course, you must have the wrist and arm to handle such rods for lengthy periods; and for many men and most women the shorter and lighter 8 or 8½ ft. fly rod is better. They may not get quite the distance or handle as heavy or bulky a lure as with the longer sticks. Yet many fish in salt water such as striped bass, bluefish, weakfish, snook, and small tarpon can be caught on shorter casts; so distance is not always a must. It is mostly needed when fishing shallow, clear waters for bonefish, channel bass, and a few other salt-water species. In order not to spook such fish, you have to cast far; and then the more powerful and longer rod is unsurpassed.

The salt-water fly rod, no matter what length is used, should have a slow action. It should bend down almost to the grip but have enough reserve power for long casts and for fighting good-sized fish. Such an action is more readily found or made in a good split-bamboo rod, so many expert fly casters fishing salt-water choose the cane rods. The Orvis impregnated salt-water fly rods are outstanding in this class. Good split-bamboo rods are expensive, and they also require more careful handling than Fiberglas rods; so the average angler settles for the glass rod. However, caution is required to obtain the right action for salt-water fly fishing with a glass rod. Too many of them have a fast, stiff action which requires too much false casting and fast timing, making it almost impossible to cast any distance with the slow-moving, bulky fly lures. One quick test to see if the rod has the right action is to hold it firmly with two hands on the cork grip and extend it in front of you. Then whip it back and forth on a horizontal plane. The rod should bend right down to the cork grip or handle.

Examine the salt-water fly rod to make sure that the snake guides are large and made of stainless steel. The reel seat should be sturdy and made of non-corrosive metal. It should also be big enough to accommodate the larger sized fly fishing reels.

There are many salmon type fly fishing reels which can also be used for salt-water fly fishing. The average sized salmon reel holding the fly line and 100 or 150 yd. of 15 lb. test backing can be used for such fish as small striped bass, small channel bass, weakfish, snook, and small tarpon. But if you go after bonefish or large tarpon, you'll need a bigger reel holding at least 200 or 250 yd. of backing line testing from 15 to 20 lb. The Fin-Nor fly reel made for very large fish and long runs has a Model No. 4, which holds 300 yd. of 27 lb. test line and the fly line.

When it comes to buying a fly reel for salt-water fishing, get the best you can afford. The cheaper reels usually lack many desirable features or are made from inferior materials. A top-quality salt-water fly reel should be made of light but strong non-corrosive metal and have a smooth, dependable, adjustable drag. It should also come apart quickly and easily for changing of spools or lubrication and cleaning. Salt-water fly reels range from about $20.00 to over $100 in price.

17

SALT-WATER LINES

Anglers seeking big fish in salt water have been plagued for centuries with the problem of finding a good, durable fishing line they could depend upon. Such early fishing line materials as horsehair, coconut, cotton, silk, and other natural animal or vegetable fibers were far from perfect. Then fishing lines were made from linen, and these were so superior to other types that they became the most widely used salt-water sport fishing lines in the United States. The earliest linen lines in this country were made by Captain Lester Crandall in 1824. He made such high quality linen fishing lines that the demand for them grew and his business flourished. Today his descendents carry on under the name of the world-famed Ashaway Line and Twine Co.

The early linen lines were made mostly by hand, being twisted with the aid of large hand-operated wheels. Today some linen lines are still being twisted by hand, but many are machine made. The best linen for fishing lines, known as "Irish" linen, is used for the highest quality lines. Although Ireland grows its own flax and uses it for lines, the best flax comes from northern France and Belgium, which have the proper climate for growing the raw products. Ireland, however, has the best spinners of linen, and the major portion of this industry is

157

located there; so flax from Belgium and France is shipped to Ireland for processing.

Linen lines are usually twisted to form what is known as "threads" and are labeled 6-thread, 9-thread, 12-thread, 15-thread and so on up to 72-thread, which is one of the heaviest used. A standard 50-lea linen line tests about 2½ lb. dry and 3 lb. wet per thread. Linen lines increase in strength when they get wet, and the wet test is generally the one which is printed on the label.

Because of this increase in strength when wet, linen lines should be thoroughly soaked before being used. Linen lines are still used quite a bit in big-game fishing and some types of bottom fishing. They are rarely used now by surf anglers who cast with conventional reels. Linen lines do have certain advantages such as lack of stretch, resistance to abrasion, and when soaked do not burn the thumb during a cast. However, linen lines also absorb water, swell, and often make casting difficult. They also tend to untwist when being trolled with lures which spin or revolve. And linen lines are also subject to rot, mildew, and general deterioration, especially if left wet on the reel. Therefore they are usually dried after each fishing trip, and even then they tend to weaken with age.

The synthetic lines such as nylon, on the other hand, are affected less by moisture, rot, and decay. They are also smaller in diameter than linen lines and do not swell much when wet; so you can get more line on the reel and make longer casts. Since nylon lines can be left on the reel wet without deteriorating, such lines are very popular with surf anglers, bait casters, and others who do a lot of casting and fishing.

The most popular nylon casting line for salt water is the braided type, usually called a "squidding" line if made for surf fishing. Such lines are usually braided to form a line without a core. Early nylon lines had too much stretch, but much of this elasticity has now been eliminated by heat treating the lines.

Nylon braided lines also vary in the softness or hardness of the braid and waterproofing; so some braided nylon lines are soft and flexible, and others are hard and stiff. The softer lines usually cast better and are easier on the thumb, but they fray more easily and do not stand abrasion. The harder lines do not fray as readily, but they burn the thumb more readily on a long cast. Nylon braided lines can be obtained in many tests, from 12 to 100 lb. or more.

Braided nylon lines are popular with surf anglers for use with conventional reels and also with many other salt-water anglers who cast artificial lures. Care must be taken when using these lines around obstructions such as rocks, coral, mussels, barnacles, etc.; for the slightest touch or rub will part braided nylon lines. And the first few feet of the line should always be examined for fraying. If it is frayed too much, you should cut off several feet and fish with a fresh section on the end.

When Du Pont put a new synthetic called dacron on the market in 1949, big-game anglers got a new line which they could use instead of the time-honored linen for offshore fishing. Dacron lines are also braided and have most of the advantages that other synthetic lines possess. In addition, they have a smaller diameter for the same pound test than nylon. Dacron lines also have less stretch than nylon lines. These qualities make them popular with offshore anglers, who need a line on their reel with a minimum of stretch for setting the hook and fighting fish at a distance.

For the same reasons, dacron lines are also popular with those who do a lot of trolling and bottom fishing, especially when bottom fishing in deep water, where a line with a lot of stretch makes it difficult to feel a bite or set the hook. Dacron lines are also used for casting but are not as popular as nylon because they are more waterproof and thus tougher on the thumb when casting long distances with heavy lures.

But braided dacron lines are slowly replacing linen lines in offshore fishing. Since they do not rot or deteriorate with age as linen lines do, they are more dependable. Dacron lines will outlast linen lines, and in the long run this makes them more economical. Dacron lines are available in 12, 20, 30, 50, 80, and 130 lb. tests.

The most versatile and widely used line in salt-water fishing today is the monofilament nylon or other mono type line. These are the single strand or filament lines which are made by the extrusion process. The first ones were put on the market by Du Pont and were called nylon or tynex lines. Today many other monofilament lines made from various chemicals are on the market.

Monofilament lines deserve their popularity because they can be used for casting, trolling, drifting, bottom fishing, or still fishing in salt water. They are especially popular with surf anglers and other salt-water fishermen who cast with spinning reels of various types, and they are economical because they outlast the natural lines such as linen by years.

Mono lines are smooth and very durable compared with linen or braided lines. They do not fray or cut as easily when rubbed against a rough surface or when used continuously for casting. They retain their strength for long periods and do not rot or weaken when used in salt water. Although nylon monofilament lines have considerable stretch, this is not objectionable unless you have a lot of line out. At the short lengths or distances, this stretch even helps you fight a fish and prevents broken lines. And mono lines are less visible in the water than linen or braided lines. When fishing in clear water or for wary fish, you can't beat the monofilament lines.

Besides being used for casting, mono lines have become very popular with bottom fishermen. For fishing with sinkers around rocks, coral, or other obstructions monofilament nylon lines take more punishment than other kinds of lines. Since mono lines have less drag and hold bottom better, their small

Dacron braided lines like this Life-Line by Ashaway come in various tests for most offshore fishing.

Cortland Cam-o-flage single strand casting monofilament is relaxed for use with casting reels.

Sunset Surf King nylon squidding line comes in tests from 12 to 110 lb. It is popular in 36 and 45 lb. tests for surf fishing.

Pfleuger Mustang plug is usel in surf fishing and boat casting and trolling for striped bass, bluefish, channel bass, tarpon, snook, and other gamefish.

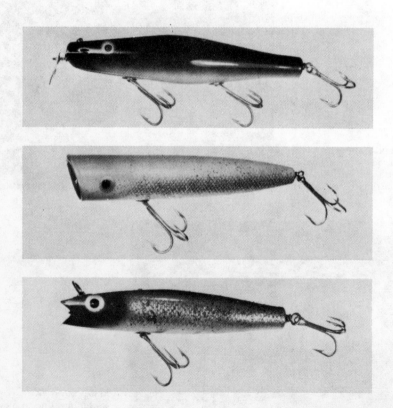

Creek Chub Surfster, *top;* "popper," center; and "darter," *bottom,* are popular with salt-water anglers for surf and boat fishing.

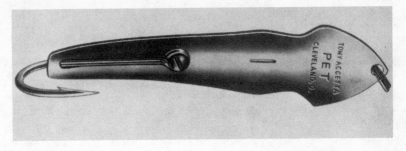

Tony Accetta Pet spoons come in vaious sizes from tiny ones for salt-water spinning to big trolling models for striped bass and offshore fishing.

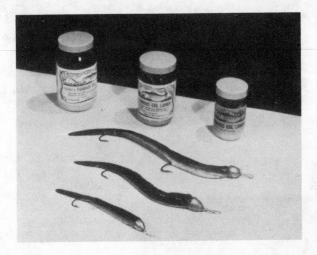

Clarke's eel lures are made from natural eels and have lead heads for easier casting or deeper trolling.

This Bill Upperman bucktail jig comes in several sizes and weights for salt-water casting and trolling The head is red and white.

This is the Florida Deep Sea Shoulder Harness sold by the Tycoon/Fin-Nor Corp.

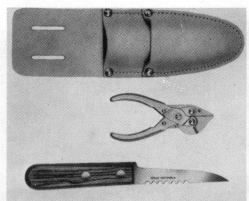

Sargent kit comes with stainless steel knife and pliers. It has many uses in salt-water fishing.

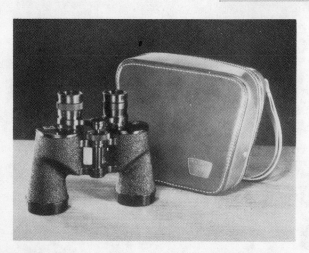

Binoculars are helpful for locating fish in salt water. These are Zephyr Light 7 x 35 for all-around use, made by Bausch & Lomb.

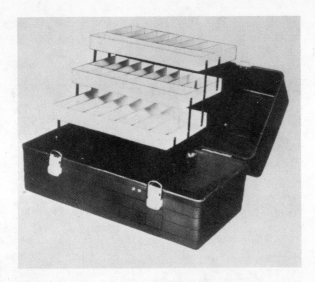

Gladding Grex tackle box is made of high density rigid polyethylene and is not affected by heat, cold, acid, oil, or salt water.

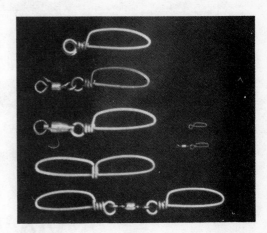

These stainless steel snaps and snap-swivels are made by Pompanette Products in various sizes.

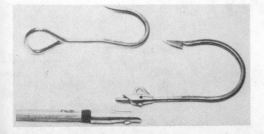

Two types of gaffs by the Tycoon/Fin-Nor Corp. The upper left shows the Meat Hook and the lower right the Flying Gaff.

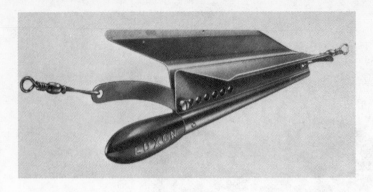

Luxon Magill stainless steel trolling planer is available in four sizes for fresh and salt-water trolling.

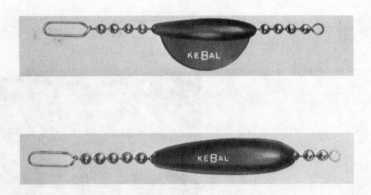

Kebal keel swivels and trolling leads come in many sizes for casting and trolling.

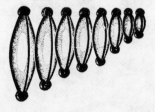

Rubbercor sinkers by the Water Gremlin Co. have rubber lined slot and tips which prevent damage to leader and line.

Basic fishing knots

IMPROVED CLINCH KNOT ... for joining line to lure

... double end back from eye of hook and take 5 turns around standing part of line

...thrust end between eye and first loop, then back through big loop as shown

... pull up slowly and tight as possible. Cut off end at one-eighth inch.

IMPROVED BLOOD KNOT ... for joining two lines

... lap ends, twist 5 times as shown, tuck end back and hold.

... Repeat at opposite end, taking 5 twists in same direction. Push end through center of lap.

... Pull up slowly and tight. Allow turns to gather as shown above.

IMPROVED END LOOP ... for forming a loop

... form a double strand 4 to 6 inches long

... fold the "U" shaped bend back and spiral around itself 5 times for maximum strength

...insert end through first loop as shown, Pull up as tight as possible.

These are the knots recommended for use with monofilament lines by the Du Pont Co.

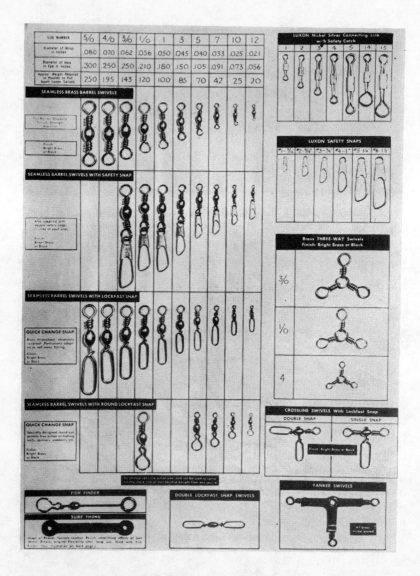

Various types of Luxon swivels, snaps, connecting links, and fish-finders made by the Art Wire and Stamping Co.

diameter and smoothness enables the bottom fishermen to use lighter sinkers.

In recent years monofilament lines have been improved to the extent that they are now used also on conventional type revolving spool reels for surf fishing or bait-casting. They are especially popular for bottom fishing in the surf or for casting artificial lures from shore or a boat. The limp monofilaments in the lighter tests can be used on such revolving spool reels, especially bait-casting reels, for both purposes.

The Stren monofilament line developed by Du Pont in recent years has also proved popular with salt-water anglers. It is supposed to have 33 per cent less original elasticity than nylon and is 20 per cent stronger for its diameter. It is also limp and flexible and doesn't spring off the reel like some of the stiffer monofilaments.

Stren monofilament lines are made in the regular round shape or the newer oval shape. The oval-shaped Stren monofilament was developed for use with conventional casting and trolling reels.

The oval lines lies flat and firm on the reel, and coils of line do not slide over or slip under one another nor spring up to cause a snarl when tension is released. Being limper than many round monofilaments of the same pound test, the oval lines do not balloon during the cast. The oval line is available in tests from 10 to 60 lb. at present.

When using monofilament lines, it is important to get a reel built especially for such lines. Such reels feature close tolerance spools, which prevent the fine monofilament line from getting behind the spool into the works.

For surface trolling, many of the lines discussed above can be used with or without lead sinkers or trolling weights. For deep trolling, however, wire lines are needed. These come in twisted, braided, single-strand, or solid types. The twisted and braided lines are somewhat easier to use and kink less than the solid wire lines. However, they have a thicker diameter and therefore do not get down as deep as the solid wire lines.

The most popular wire line for salt-water trolling today is the solid wire Monel (nickel alloy) line. Anywhere from 100 to 300 feet of this line is used in shallow water trolling, while even greater lengths can be used for deep trolling. It can be obtained in tests from 5 to 85 lb., with those testing 30 to 50 lb. the most popular sizes for salt-water fishing. Usually more than half the reel is filled with linen or braided backing line first, and the wire line is added on top of that.

When using wire line, constant care is necessary to prevent loose coils on the reel or kinks in the line itself. When letting wire line off the reel spool, put the click of the reel on so that it runs off smoothly. If a kink develops in the line, try to straighten it out before it gets worse. If the kink is very bad, the line may have to be cut and spliced. Wire lines will wear ordinary guides on a rod, so most anglers prefer the roller guides and tip-tops.

Fly lines used in salt water should be made of nylon and should match the rod being used. This usually means a weight-forward or bug taper fly line in the GBF or GAF sizes for most 9 to 9½ ft. fly rods. There should be enough backing of braided nylon or dacron line in the 15 to 20 lb. tests to handle the fish you are seeking.

Care should be taken in spooling the line you buy on the reel to avoid twists or kinks. Some tackle dealers will spool the line on the reel by machine if they have this accomodation. If you do it yourself, make sure that the line is packed on the reel spool firmly but not too tight. Nor should it be too loose. This job is best accomplished by having one man hold the line spools and apply tension while the other man cranks the line on the reel. Most line holders have a hold through which you can run a pencil or other round rod for fast, smooth removal of the line.

18
SALT-WATER LURES

The use of artificial lures for sport fishing in salt water is a relatively recent development. It's true that some anglers used them and caught fish in salt water in Europe and this country during the 1800's. But they were a mere handful of pioneers, and the great majority of salt-water anglers used natural baits. The picture began to change after 1900, when more and more manufacturers began making fresh-water lures. Many of these were also used in salt water with good results. But it is mainly in the last twenty five years that salt-water anglers began to make extensive use of artificial lures.

The earliest lures used in salt-water fishing were mostly cedar or bone jigs, metal squids, Jap feathers or fresh-water spoons, spinners, and plugs. Many of the fresh-water lures can be used in salt water, especially for the smaller species. But in the long run, it is more economical and practical to use lures made especially for salt-water fishing. These are usually larger, heavier, and have stronger hooks and fittings to take the wear and tear of larger fish and salt-water rust and corrosion.

Before World War II is was often difficult to find good salt-water lures made especially for salt-water fishing. But after the War many fishing lure companies started making lures designed for taking salt-water species. Now there is a wide variety of such lures in almost any well-stocked coastal fishing tackle store.

One of the oldest artificial lures used for surf fishing and trolling is the metal squid. Squids come in dozens of different sizes, shapes, and weights. Most of them imitate some short, broad fish such as a mullet, anchovy, menhaden, or herring. A few metal squids are long and narrow and simulate baitfish such as sand eels, spearing, or silversides, and salt-water minnows of various kinds.

Metal squids are made from lead, block tin, and other metals. Block tin squids are popular, and they stay shiny and bright or can be quickly polished with steel wool. Other metals usually have to be chrome or nickel plated since they are dull or tarnish quickly.

Usually one hook is used in metal squids, and this may be imbedded in the squid or attached so that it swings. The plain metal squid will often catch fish; but most anglers add a strip of pork rind or tie white, yellow, or red feathers or hair around the hook.

Metal squids will run in weight from small ones of $1/4$ oz. up to 4 or 5 oz. The smaller, lighter ones are best for small fish and light casting outfits when fishing from shore, surf, or boats. The larger, heavier metal squids are better for big fish and heavier fishing outfits. Although primarily casting lures used from surf or boats, metal squids can also be trolled to take a wide variety of salt-water species. They are especially effective for striped bass, bluefish, channel bass, weakfish, and other predatory gamefish.

Each metal squid has a different action and depth at which it works best. Some come in fairly straight, while others sway violently from side to side. Reeling at a moderate speed will usually bring out the best action. But sometimes fast reeling will produce more strikes; other times slow reeling is best. You can often improve the action of a lead or block tin squid by bending it.

Spoons are also widely used in salt-water fishing. Many of the smaller spoons used in fresh-water fishing can also be used in salt water, especially for the smaller species and when casting with the lighter outfits. However, the spoons made for salt-water fishing are usually heavier, thicker, and equipped with stronger hooks. Most spoons are oval or fish-like in shape and dished or bent to provide a wobbling or swaying action. They come in brass, copper, nickel, chrome, gold, or silver finishes. Stainless steel spoons and the nickel, silver, or chrome finishes are usually best in salt water. There are times, however, when other finishes or colors produce, too. Many spoons are painted on one or both sides in white, yellow, red, or other colors.

For small fish and light outfits, the spoons running from about 1½ to 3 in. in length equipped with treble or single hooks can be used for casting or trolling. These usually run up to an ounce or so in weight. The larger spoons, from 3 to 8 in., can be used for bigger fish in trolling. In recent years big spoons up to 12 in. long and 4 in. wide have become popular in trolling for striped bass. These so-called "bunker" spoons are made to imitate the bunker or menhaden. However, various companies make many other large spoons which can also be used for striped bass, channel bass, big bluefish, and other large salt-water fish. These are usually equipped with big, husky salt-water hooks going from 8/0 to 12/0 or larger.

In recent years the Hopkins "No-Eql" spoon-type lure has proven deadly for such fish as striped bass, bluefish, channel bass, pollock, barracuda, bonito, and dolphin. This is a flat lure with rippled, multi-mirrored sides which glitter and shine. It is made of solid stainless steel and comes in various sizes and weights for casting and trolling from boats or surf.

When using spoons, slow reeling or trolling usually produces the best results. An erratic retrieve works on many occasions when casting and reeling. Here you jerk the rod tip, then pause, let the spoon sink and flutter, then speed up or jerk again, repeating this during the entire retrieve. This imitates a crippled baitfish and often brings a smashing strike. Spoons are usually best during the daytime although they'll occasionally take fish at night.

Spinners also take their share of salt-water fish. Like the spoons they depend on flash and motion to attract fish. In this respect the two are similar. The revolving blade may also give off vibrations which attract fish. Spinners are made to revolve on a wire shaft, and the blades may vary in number. Usually one or two are used, but when trolling for salmon in the Pacific Northwest, several may be lined up in a series.

Spinners come in various finishes and metals; but the silver, nickel, chrome, or stainless steel finishes are usually preferred for salt-water use. The blades may be round, oval, or leaf-shaped. Spinners will catch fish when used alone, but they are generally combined on trailing hooks with various baits including seaworms, strips of squid, pork rind, or baitfish. Two popular types used in salt-water are the June Bug and Cape Cod spinners. The latter is a consistent taker of small striped bass when trolled with blood worms or sandworms on the hooks. The so-called "fluke" and "snapper" spinners consist of two blades and are used with small baitfish such as killies or with spearing for trolling or bottom drifting.

Spinners should be trolled very slowly at varying depths until the fish are located. They can also be let out in the current from a bridge, pier, or boat and worked slowly back against the current. For bottom fish and some gamefish, they can be trolled very slowly near the bottom with a sinker. Or the boat can drift with the wind and tide just fast enough to turn over the blades.

When it comes to plugs, we find that there are now many different salt-water types on the market. Here again, many fresh-water plugs can be used for salt-water fishing. But those made especially for salt-water use are larger, heavier, and stronger. The hooks, especially, should be of strong, heavy wire. Weak hooks are quickly straightened by big fish or soon rust and break. There are still many good wooden plugs on the market, but more and more plastic body plugs are appearing each year. They are more durable and have more permanent colors.

The surface type plugs are made to create a ripple, splash or commotion on the top of the water to attract fish. These plugs include the poppers, swimmers, and torpedo shapes which stay on top during most of the retrieve. Surface plugs come in varying sizes, from 3 in. for small fish and light outfits up to 12 in. for big jointed-eel jobs. They have cupped or dished heads, metal lips, propellers, or pointed noses, which disturb the water in some way or give the plug body a fish-like movement. They are made to imitate such baitfish as herring, menhaden, mullet, spearing, sardines, or shiners swimming on top. These plugs usually have two or three treble hooks attached to the body.

Most natural color scale finishes are good in surface plugs, although all-white, all-yellow, or transparent plugs also work well. But action is more important than color when it comes to surface plugs. Some have a built-in action, and straight reeling will often bring strikes. But others, such as the poppers or torpedo shapes, must be jerked at regular intervals to create a splash or commotion. The idea is to imitate a frantic baitfish seeking to escape from a larger gamefish. Surface plugs are usually used in surf fishing or casting inshore from a boat for striped bass, bluefish, and other fish which feed on top.

Another deadly salt-water plug is the darter type, which has a notched head and tapering body. The smaller ones are similar to those used in fresh water and are good with light spinning or bait-casting outfits. The larger darters are usually loaded

with lead near the tail for easier casting in the surf. Darters can
be worked by reeling straight and making the plug dart just
under the surface, or they can be reeled slowly and twitched
with pauses on the surface. The Creek Chub and Stan Gibbs
darters are favorite lures of this type and come in various sizes
and weights.

Underwater plugs are widely used in salt-water fishing. Most
of these float on the surface until reeled or pulled, when they
dive to various depths and wriggle from side to side. These
usually have a metal lip of some type to give the plug action
and make it dive to the desire depth. Some have blunt or
pointed heads which do not give them any kind of action but
must be worked with the rod tip to give them a fishy dart and
pause movement.

Underwater plugs come in various sizes, shapes, and weights,
measuring from 3 to 10 in. in length and weighing anywhere
from ½ oz. up to 4 or 5 oz. They usually come in white, yellow,
or red and white, or natural scale finishes. They all produce
results, depending on the condition of the water, the baitfish
present, and the gamefish being sought.

Underwater plugs can be reeled in without any rod action
if they have a built-in wriggle, dart, or wobble. But even these
produce better at times if jerked at regular intervals, stopped,
slowed down, or speeded up for variety. In shallow water they
can be reeled more slowly so they don't dive too deep. But in
deeper waters they are reeled faster. Try to feel the plug working—if you can't, reel in to see if it has picked up weeds or has
become fouled. Underwater plugs can be cast from the surf,
shore, or boats, or trolled for a wide variety of salt-water species.

The most versatile lures a spinning angler can use in salt
water are jigs. Also called bucktails, bugeyes, bullheads, and
barracudas, these deadly lures are consistent producers. They
are compact and can be cast like a bullet on light lines. They
sink fast and can be fished at almost any depth by casting or

trolling. Best of all, they appeal to most fish, often catching bottom species as well as gamefish. They are especially effective in southern waters but also catch fish in northern waters.

Jigs come in different weights, colors, sizes, and dressings. Most of them are similar in that they have a heavy lead or other metal head with feathers, bucktail or other hair, nylon, rubber, or plastic skirts wrapped around the hook. The metal head is chromed or painted in various colors. Those with white, yellow, or red heads predominate in salt-water fishing.

Most jigs range in weight from ⅛ oz. up to 3 or 4 oz. The single hooks molded into the head run from sizes 6 up to 8/0. The heaviest ones are used for casting or trolling with heavier outfits, while the smaller ones are used with light outfits.

Jigs are used both in casting and trolling from shore or boats. They are trolled fast for such speedsters as small tuna, albacore, bonito, and mackerel. For other fish, a moderate or slow speed is better. The rod tip should be jerked at regular intervals while trolling.

When used for fishing from the surf, small boats, bridges, and piers, jigs can be adapted to conditions and the water being fished. When fish are feeding on the surface chasing baitfish, the jig is cast out and immediately reeled in fairly fast or at a moderate speed. On other occasions it can be cast out, allowed to sink a few feet, then jerked, allowed to sink, jerked, etc. It can also be cast out, then slowly bounced along the bottom all the way in. Other times you can lower the jig to the bottom and "jig" or work it up and down so that it dances around just off the bottom. In a current it can often be cast across and slightly upstream, then allowed to drift down and sink as it is carried downstream. Jigs are excellent lures in fast currents and deep water since they sink quickly and offer less resistance to the water than other lures. When used with light spinning lines they enable an angler to fish depths seldom reached with most lures.

A good assortment of jigs in various sizes and colors is a must for salt-water spinning, as well as for trolling. They take up little room, and a dozen or two can be carried in a small tackle box. You need plenty, too, because jigs often get hung up on the bottom and are lost.

Somewhat similar to jigs are the Jap feather type trolling lures, which have shiny metal heads with a hole through which a wire leader is run and a hook is attached. They have skirts of feathers, bucktail, nylon, or saran, in white, yellow, red, green, blue, or combos of these. Feather lures come in many sizes and weights, from ⅛ oz. for small fish and light tackle up to 16 oz. for big-game fish. The larger sizes are used in fast trolling for tuna, marlin, sharks, bonito, albacore, king mackerel, dolphin, and similar offshore species.

Another similar lure to the Jap feather or jig is the longer eel jig, which has a nylon or saran tail up to 12 in. long. It is usually rigged with two hooks and is used for trolling for striped bass, bluefish, and other fish.

Still another lure called a "jig" is the diamond jig, which has four flat sides and a treble hook attached to the tail. Some of these jigs may also have a single hook imbedded in the body of the jig. The smaller ones with the single hook, usually called weakfish or mackerel jigs, are used for these fish. But the most common type of diamond jig has treble hooks and bright, shiny nickel or chrome finishes. They come in various sizes from 1 to 10 oz. and are deadly for all kinds of game and bottom fish. These jigs can be cast and reeled or trolled behind a boat to catch fish. But the best way to use them is to let them down to the bottom, and when they hit, quickly yank them up, and then let them settle again. Such "jigging" will catch almost anything that swims in the ocean.

Then there are eelskin lures, which have weighted heads and two trailing hooks on a chain or wire. An eelskin turned inside out is tied to the head; and when this is cast and reeled or trolled, the skin inflates. The metal heads in front are hollow or have holes which permit the water to enter and inflate the skin. The heads come in various weights, usually from 1 to 3 oz. Eelskin lures are favorites for trolling or casting for striped bass and bluefish but will also take other salt-water fish at times. They are usually worked with jerks at regular intervals and will take fish during the day or night. The rigs and eelskins can be bought separately in most fishing tackle stores.

Somewhat similar are the rigged eels or eel tails, which run from 6 to 20 in. in length. They are rigged with one or two hooks, one usually near the head and the other near the tail. The eel bob types have the head of the eel removed and a lead weight inserted under the skin. Other anglers add metal plates or small metal squids at the head of the eel to provide casting weight or action. Eels are used mainly at night but will take fish occasionally in the daytime. They are reeled or trolled at slow speeds for striped bass. In recent years the larger rigged eels have been used offshore, where they are trolled fast for such fish as marlin. Most anglers rig their own eels, but prepared eels can often be bought in coastal tackle stores, either frozen or packed in jars with a preservative.

For fly fishing in salt water, various kinds of big flies are used. These are usually gaudy and tied on large No. 1, 1/0, 2/0, or 3/0 hooks. The O'Shaughnessy hook is preferred because of its strength, and those made of Z nickel do not rust and ruin the hair or feathers. Most of the flies are streamers or bucktails, but some are of the bass bug type with wood or cork heads and hair or feather tails. The most popular colors are white, yellow, red, light blue, or combinations of these. They are supposed to imitate small baitfish such as spearing or silversides, mullet, herring, anchovies, or shiners. Some look more like small salt-water shrimp. The popper type surface flies or bugs are retrieved with jerks to throw a spray. The streamers or bucktails are worked just below the surface in long sweeps and pauses to simulate a baitfish swimming. Salt-water flies will catch striped bass, channel bass, bluefish, weakfish and sea trout, mackerel, albacore, bonito, snappers, and many other species.

There are also many rubber and plastic imitation lures for use in salt-water fishing. These are usually lifelike representations of such creatures as minnows or baitfish, eels, seaworms, shrimp, and squid. Usually soft and flexible, most of them have no built-in action but must be worked with the rod tip when casting or jerked occasionally when trolled.

Finally, we have pork rind or strips, which are used mostly in combination with other lures. There are strips of various widths, lengths, and thicknesses to add to metal squids, jigs, spoons, and plugs. Most of the pork rind strips are plain, but some have a single hook attached to catch the short strikers. In recent years longer and wider pork rind strips have been made for use in offshore trolling for the larger big-game fish. These may be up to 10 or 12 in. long, a couple of inches wide, and 1/4 in. thick. Pork rind strips come packed in jars and can be obtained in white, yellow, or red.

19

SALT-WATER ACCESSORIES

Like the fresh-water angler, the salt-water angler also has a long list of accessories from which to choose to make his fishing, safer, more comfortable, and productive. One of the most evident differences between an amateur or casual salt-water angler and a real veteran is the number of accessories each carries. The novice usually brings a rod, reel, line, hooks or lures, and a few scattered items. But the veteran usually comes loaded down with one or more big tackle boxes or bags with a wide variety of accessory items which help make his fishing trip a success. When you are fishing a lonely beach or out in a boat miles from shore, you can't rush back and get something that you need desperately. So the wise salt-water angler brings everything he thinks he will need that day or may need in an emergency.

If you plan to do any wading in the surf, bays, rivers, or other salt water, you'll need a pair of hip boots or waders. If the surf isn't too rough and you don't step into water over the boot tops, you can use rubber boots. Many anglers fishing from the beaches or jetties wear a pair of rubber overalls over the boots. This helps keep the spray or a sudden wave from filling the boots. But you can't wade out too far with hip boots.

Most surf anglers prefer a pair of waders for surf fishing from sand beaches, rock jetties, and rocky shores. These are not only more waterproof but also warmer in cold weather. For surf fishing, a pair of all-rubber waders which come up to the armpits are best for all-around use. They are rugged, waterproof, and comfortable on the colder spring and fall days and nights. When worn while fishing on sandy beaches or during the hot summer months, the plastic waders are lighter and more comfortable. But they don't stand up very well when used on rock jetties or along rocky shores. The canvas type waders with a layer of rubber between them can be used, but they tend to stay damp inside and out and do not dry as fast as the all-rubber types.

When buying waders for surf fishing, make sure that there is plenty of room in the crotch and for the feet. You have to do a lot of walking and rock-hopping on jetties or rocky shores; so you should have plenty of room for lifting your legs. There should also be enough room for your feet with a pair of heavy wool socks or two or three pairs of lighter ones.

Some kind of waterproof jacket is also required by surf and boat anglers. Surf anglers usually wear a parka type waterproof jacket with hood. This should be light but have tight seams, drawstrings at the waist and neck, and cuffs which can be drawn tightly or buttoned snugly. When such a parka is worn over a pair of waders, it keeps you dry and comfortable in a rain or when the waves are splashing.

Boat fishermen also use waterproof jackets on cold, windy days; when the spray is flying; or on rainy days. The same type of parka jacket with hood is good, but this should be matched with a pair of waterproof pants which can be worn with the jacket. A short pair of boots up to the ankles or knees can also be worn with this to keep your feet dry on a wet deck. When you're chumming from a boat, a pair of rubber overalls can't be beat to keep you dry and clean.

Salt-water anglers also need some kind of hat or cap to protect them from the elements. The long-peaked caps are light and are preferred by most surf anglers and offshore fishermen to keep the sun out of their eyes. In southern or tropical waters, such hats fail to keep the sun from burning your neck or top of your ears, so many anglers fishing all day in such waters like a light hat with a wide brim. When surf or boat fishing during the early spring, late fall, or in the winter, a warm wool hunting type hat with lining and ear flaps is a great comfort.

Surf anglers climbing over slippery rocks and jetties need something on their feet to keep them from taking a fall. They use ice-creepers, hobnails, chains, and various types of home-made sandals for this. You can also buy rubber sandals with felt soles, which can be attached to your boots or waders. These usually work fine on rocks; but when fishing on wood jetties or inclined mossy rocks, some kind of hobnails or points should be used to grip and hold the wood or rocks.

Surf anglers also need a pouch or bag in which to carry their lures and other items. Big shoulder bags and knapsacks are fine when you are fishing one or two spots and don't expect to move around much. These bags are roomy and have compartments or pockets for lures, hooks, sinkers, rigs, bait, and even a lunch. But when a surf angler plans to fish rock jetties or walk up and down a beach or rocky shore for long distances, he needs something smaller and lighter. Small shoulder bags can be bought. Most veteran anglers, however, prefer the small bags or pouches which can be slipped over an Army type web pistol belt or heavy leather belt and worn outside the other clothing at the waist. Many of these pouches can be bought in an Army and Navy surplus goods store. Other bags with compartments for large plugs and metal squids can be bought and attached to the belt.

Boat fishermen fishing salt waters usually have some kind of tackle box for their gear. The big, all wood tackle boxes with many compartments for lures, a reel or two, and other items are fine if you don't have to carry them too far or too often. So are some of the plastic tackle boxes on the market. There are also aluminum boxes which can be used for salt-water tackle. The only trouble is that it is hard to find a salt-water tackle box which will hold some of the big plugs, spoons, and other lures used in salt-water fishing. Most of the tackle boxes on the market have short, narrow compartments which are good for small or medium sized lures but not for the largest types.

Boat anglers also need a landing net or gaff. It the fish are small or difficult to gaff, like the fluke, a net is usually best. For salt-water fishing, the landing net should have a long handle and wide opening. There are many such nets with aluminum frames and handles on the market. For big fish a gaff is usually better; and, of course, for the big-game fish a gaff is the only thing that can be used. Gaffs have long handles, the length depending on the type of boat from which you are fishing. Rowboats and skiffs call for shorter gaffs than those on cruisers or party boats. For offshore fishing, a big flying gaff is often needed. Here the hook is attached to a strong line and detached from the handle when an active fish is gaffed.

Surf anglers use long-handled gaffs from jetties, breakwaters, and other spots high above the water. When beach fishing or wading in the water, they use the small, short-handled gaffs which can be carried on the person. These can be bought; or, by buying the gaff hook in any tackle store and wrapping heavy cord or wire around the hook and a wooden handle, you can make your own. Many surf anglers prefer the pick or strike type of gaff, which has the point bent out instead of parallel to the shank, as in most gaffs. These short gaffs are usually attached to an elastic cord and are worn on the belt in a protected sheath for instant use.

Many of the larger boats have fish boxes in which to keep fish which are caught. On the smaller boats the round plastic containers used for garbage or trash will often serve the purpose. These usually have a cover, handle, and room for a chunk of ice to keep the fish or bait fresh.

Surf anglers use fish stringers to hold fish or drag them along the beach in shallow water. The fresh-water type stringers are usually too short for this; so most surf anglers make their own, using 8 to 12 ft. lengths of clothesline or nylon cord.

For help in fighting a fish, surf anglers often wear a rod belt with cup around the waist. When bait fishing, the small cup-type rod belt is sufficient, but when fishing at night or when squidding with artificial lures, the larger rod belts with a wide leather apron are better. Offshore anglers, of course, need a harness of some type to help fight the big ones they hook. There are two types in common use: the shoulder harness and the kidney harness. The shoulder harness rests high on your shoulders and back and gives you plenty of leverage for fighting and pumping a fish. However, this type of harness requires a well-developed back and plenty of physical strength. Not everyone can use it as effectively as the other type: the kidney harness. This harness, as the name implies, fits around the lower part of your back and is more comfortable and easier to use. Therefore it is preferred by most beginners, and many expert anglers also like it.

Boat anglers and surf anglers need some kind of portable light which can be available at all times. On a large boat a searchlight or large portable light with handle will often serve the purpose. However, for the surf angler and the small boat angler, a headlight is best. This is the type with an elastic band attached to the lamp, which goes around your head or neck. A cords runs from the lamp to a battery case, which is slipped in your pocket or is worn on your belt. Such a light leaves your hands free for running a boat, casting, playing a fish from the beach or rocks, and for any other purpose.

Every salt-water angler requires a knife at one time or another, and this should always be carried on the person. For this, a pocket knife made of stainless steel with a long blade and hook disgorger, bottle opener, and fish scaler can't be beat. Many surf anglers and offshore fishermen also like a large, hunting sheath knife, which can be carried on the belt for instant use. And, of course, for filleting and cleaning fish, a good fillet knife with a long blade is a must.

Cutting and gripping pliers also come in handy on many occasions. There are combination types on the market which make it possible to carry only one pair for most needs. But there are other types such as round-nosed pliers which are also good for making wire leaders. In fact, a kit with most of the tools needed for light repair jobs can be carried in a large boat or should be available in the car for emergencies.

A good pair of sunglasses can save your eyes from damage by protecting them from the rays and glare of the sun on the water or the beach. Surf anglers need them if they fish much during the daytime, and boat anglers can use them almost every day except on very cloudy days. Sunglasses need not be expensive but should have the correct shade of glass or plastic to cut out most of the harmful rays.

In addition to the sunglasses, a tube or jar of sun-tan lotion should be taken along to protect the face, neck, arms, and hands if the sun is very bright. And when fishing during the summer months up north or in southern waters, an insect repellent is also needed.

Surf anglers and boat anglers can also use a good pair of binoculars for spotting birds working or feeding on fish and also to detect activity among the other boats as a clue to the presence of fish. The binoculars should be small and light and not too strong if used on a boat. The vibrations from the motor will shake them and make it difficult to see. Binoculars should be carried in a tough, waterproof case.

There are also other odds and ends which can be taken along on most fishing trips, such as oil and sharpening stone for the reels and hooks, scales to weigh fish, fishing gloves, and a picnic bag or refrigerator box for keeping food and drinks cool and fresh. Most fishing trips are some distance from your home, and it's better to bring too much stuff even if you don't use some of it than to find out you need something badly but forgot to bring it.

20
HOOKS

One of the smallest items of fishing tackle used in fresh and salt-water angling is the ordinary fishhook. But tiny though it is, the hook is one of the most important and vital links of equipment in the entire chain of fishing gear. When you come right down to it, the rod, reel, line, and lure are used mainly to get the hook within reach of a fish. Only the hook makes actual contact with the fish. All the parts of a fishing outfit are important, of course. Rod, reel, line, and lure should all play their parts in catching a fish. But the best and strongest fishing outfit is useless if the hook on the end fails to do its job.

Yet it is surprising how few fresh and salt-water anglers really make a deep study of the common fishhook. They can usually talk for hours about rods, reels, lines, and lures. But when it comes to hooks, anglers usually dismiss them with a few words. Or they rarely give much thought to the hook on the end of their line or on their lures.

The exceptions are the veteran or expert anglers. They have learned through bitter experience that they can't neglect the all-important fishhook. They know that you rarely lose a big fish or any fish because the rod breaks or the reel doesn't work or the line parts. These things happen, of course, but not too often. Most of the time when a fish is lost it either fails to get hooked, throws the hook, straighens it out, or snaps it off; so

180

most veteran anglers pay close attention to their hooks. Some are downright fussy about the style or pattern, size, and quality of the hooks they use. But all anglers can benefit from a closer study of fishhooks.

There's nothing modern about most of the fishhooks used today. In recent times only a few radical changes or innovations have been brought about. Most of the hooks used today have changed little in design from those used hundreds or even thousands of years ago. Most of the improvements which have been made are in the quality of the steel, the temper, and finish of the hook. The older hooks were cruder and less uniform and often undependable.

The development of the modern fishhook was gradual and carried out over a long period spanning thousands of years. The earliest so-called "hooks" used by prehistoric peoples were nothing more than short lengths of bone, stone, or wood sharpened on both ends to a point. A line was tied near the center of this primitive hook, which was called a gorge. It was then buried inside a bait. When a fish swallowed the whole works, the gorge set crosswise in its mouth, throat, or stomach, and held him.

The next development was the double hook, which was made from soft metal, bent in the middle, and curved on both ends. Then it was discovered that a hook with a single curve worked just as well. Such curved hooks without barbs were used by the Egyptians during the First Dynasty between 5702 B.C. and 2700 B.C. Finally, more than 3000 years ago, someone added a barb to the hook; and we had a fishhook very similar to the one we use today.

It wasn't until the fifteenth century, however, that fishhooks were made on a large scale. At that time some English needle makers decided to manufacture hooks in large quantities. They succeeded and from England the secrets of fishhook making were carried to Norway and Sweden. Now fishhooks are made in England, Norway, Germany, France, Belgium, Japan, and the United States. In the United States the fishhook industry dates back to 1864, when the American Fish Hook Company began making hooks. This company was absorbed by the Enterprise Manufacturing Co., which still makes fishhooks and the well-known Pflueger line of fishing tackle. Other large manufacturers in this country are the Wright & McGill Co. of Denver, Colorado, and the Auburn Fishhook Co. of Auburn, New York.

The early fishhooks in England and Norway were made mostly by hand, and production was slow. Today, ingenious automatic machines turn out hooks by the millions in a short time. The machine takes the wire from the coil, cleans it, straightens it, cuts it to lengths, cuts the barb, mills and grinds the point, forges, bends the hook to shape, and forms the eye in a rapid continuous operation. These remarkable machines can be adjusted so that any desired bend, wire size, and any size hook from the smallest to the largest can be made. Finally, the hooks are hardened, tempered, finished, and packaged. While most hooks are made by machine today, there still some hooks such as extra-fine fly hooks and large big-game hooks which require hand work.

Although more and more hooks are being made in the United States, we still import large quantities, mostly from Norway, England, France, and Japan. The O. Mustad & Son Co. of Oslo, Norway, is one of the largest fishhook manufacturers in the world. Norwegian made hooks are fairly cheap but are well-made and are widely used, not only by anglers but also by commercial fishermen. English fishhooks are among the best in the world and are especially noted for their fine needle points. Many of their hooks, however, are brittle and snap more readily than those made in other countries. French hooks are not imported in very large quantities; but their small, fine-wire treble hooks are popular for small fishing lures.

Japanese hooks in the past, have varied in quality and were often poorly made and undependable. But efforts are being made to improve all Japanese products slated for export and there is no reason why Japan can't make top-notch fishhooks. Their best cameras are now considered equal or superior to those made anywhere else in the world. So if they decide to go after the fishhook market—look out!

Before anyone can understand fishhooks he must know something about their various parts and construction. Hooks vary a great deal in size, design and construction of the point, shank, bend, and eye. Take the shank for example. Most hooks have the regular length shank for a particular size. As a rule the regular length shank is best for most fishing purposes, but there are times when other lengths are used. Almost any pattern of hook can be made in short or long shank.

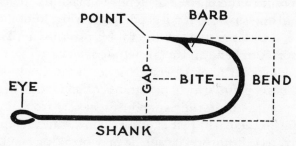

Parts of a hook

Short shanks are often used for tying such flies as spiders and variants. Hooks with short shanks are also used for bait fishing so that the hook is less visible or can be buried inside the bait. Such hooks are often used with salmon eggs or when using live sardines or anchovies in the Pacific for albacore or yellowtail.

Long-shanked hooks are commonly used for tying such flies as streamers or bucktails. They are also used for fish which tend to swallow the bait or have sharp teeth which could cut through a line or nylon leader.

Hook shanks are usually straight and of even thickness. But there are variations, as, for example, small hooks used for tying dry flies, which often have tapered shanks and eyes. This reduces the weight of the hook, which is an important factor in a dry-fly hook. Shanks may also have humps on hooks which are used for making bass bugs and other lures. Or the shanks may have slices (small barbs) which hold natural baits such as worms better along the entire length of the hook.

The point on a hook may also vary. One of the commonest points in use is the spear, which is in a straight line from point to barb. Such a point requires force to penetrate and may not go beyond the barb if it isn't set with force or if it strikes the hard part of a fish's mouth. This point is found on most hooks since it is easily made by machine.

A hollow point hook is rounded out or dished out from tip of the point to the barb. This tends to make the point somewhat thin and shallow. It is a good penetrating point and holds well in fish with soft mouths. But for big fish with hard mouths, it may spring or bend and not penetrate as well.

A needle-point hook is what is called a fast hook—it has a needle-sharp point which penetrates quickly and deeply. A needle point is uniformly round as it tapers from the tip of the point to the barb. If it is properly made and tempered, it is strong, too. If not well made, it may break or bend.

The rolled-in point is bent in toward the shank and resembles a claw, talon, or beak. Such a point tends to take a shallower bite and doesn't penetrate quite as quickly or easily as a straight point. However, once it has set beyond the barb, it holds well and is difficult to disgorge or throw. This point is very popular with live bait fishermen in fresh and salt water.

The eye on a hook may be ball, tapered, looped, or needle. The ball or ringed eye is the most common. The wire is bent into a circle, and the thickness of the wire is the same diameter throughout. On a tapered eye the end of the wire forming the ring decreases in diameter and is thinner than the rest of the hook. Such tapered eyes are found mostly on hooks used to tie dry flies. The tapered eye reduces the weight of the hook and makes it possible to tie more delicate flies. However, it is also used at times for salt-water hooks where the eye would be too big if it weren't tapered. Such tapering weakens the hook, of course; and the eye may break or open under heavy strain.

The looped eye is more or less oval shaped and runs back along the hook shank, where the end may be tapered. A needle eye, as the name implies, is similar to the eye found on needles. Some hooks are also made without eyes and instead have only tapered ends or knobbed, marked, or flatted shanks. Such hooks are used mostly for tying snelled hooks. Eyes can be turned up away from the point to provide more gap room. Such "turned-up" eyes are usually found on small, short-shanked hooks. The eye may also be "turned down" toward the point. This type of hook is used for tying flies and hooks on leaders or snells for baitfishing.

The bend or curved part of a hook also varies according to the pattern or design. Some hooks are made with a round bend. These usually have a wide gap (the space between the point and the shank of the hook). Other hooks have bends with various angles, and in some of these the angle is so sharp that the gap is very narrow.

The bend of the hook can be offset or kirbed. If you hold the point of the hook towards you and the shank on the far side, an offset hook will have the point facing either to the left or right. Such hooks are not popular for artificial lures but are widely used for live bait fishing in fresh and salt water.

The temper of a hook is a vital factor which usually separates the cheap hooks from the expensive ones. On a cheap hook the temper may be too brittle or too soft, both disadvantages. A hook that is too brittle snaps or breaks when it hits a hard object or when under strain while fighting a big fish. A hook

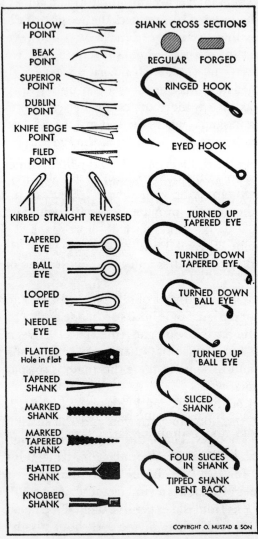

HOLLOW POINT

BEAK POINT

SUPERIOR POINT

DUBLIN POINT

KNIFE EDGE POINT

FILED POINT

KIRBED   STRAIGHT   REVERSED

TAPERED EYE

BALL EYE

LOOPED EYE

NEEDLE EYE

FLATTED
Hole in flat

TAPERED SHANK

MARKED SHANK

MARKED TAPERED SHANK

FLATTED SHANK

KNOBBED SHANK

SHANK CROSS SECTIONS

REGULAR   FORGED

RINGED HOOK

EYED HOOK

TURNED UP TAPERED EYE

TURNED DOWN TAPERED EYE

TURNED DOWN BALL EYE

TURNED UP BALL EYE

SLICED SHANK

FOUR SLICES IN SHANK

TIPPED SHANK BENT BACK

COPYRIGHT O. MUSTAD & SON

Different kinds of points and eyes found on hooks

that is too soft straightens out too easily and fails to hold a big fish. As a general rule, for most fresh and salt-water fishing for the smaller species, it is best to have a hook which gives a bit rather than a brittle one which snaps or breaks. You may lose an occasional fish which straightens a hook out, but you can quickly bend it back into shape and land the next fish. A flexible hook can also be saved if it gets caught on an underwater obstruction, but too brittle a hook which breaks at the barb or bend is useless and must be replaced.

Hooks come in many finishes including Japanned, bronzed, blued, nickel-plated, silver-plated, gold-plated, tinned, and cadmium-plated. The cheapest hooks are usually bronzed or blued. Hooks with these finishes, while satisfactory for freshwater fishing, rust quickly in salt water. After you use them once or twice, they should be discarded. Inexpensive Japanned hooks which are coated with black metal or lacquer, resist rust effectively for a long time. Such hooks are popular for bait fishing in fresh water and for commercial fishing in salt water. Nickel-plated hooks are fine for fresh water but rust quickly in salt water. They also glitter too much for wary fish but may act as attractors on artificial lures. Gold-plated hooks have a very durable thin plating of gold, which lasts a long time. They have become very popular for artificial lures and for bait-fishing in salt water. They are a bit more expensive but are worth the price since the same hook may be used many times. Tinned hooks and cadmium-plated hooks are also popular for salt-water fishing since they do not rust too quickly.

For salt-water fishing the so-called "Z" nickel hooks sold by the Auburn Fishhook Company are popular. They don't corrode or rust in salt water and are being used more and more for artificial lures. They don't stain feathers, hair, or nylon on such lures as steel hooks do. And they don't rust or corrode in a fishing tackle box. They are more expensive than regular hooks but are worth the price when used on artificial lures over and over again.

Hook sizes are often confusing. The numbers fail to give a clear picture of the length and width of a hook unless you have had a lot of experience with the hooks in various sizes of a particular pattern. The numbers start with 22 as one of the smallest and run down the line to 20, 18, 16, 14, 12, 10, 8, 6, 4, 2, 1, as they increase in size. After number 1 the hooks run 1/0, 2/0, 3/0, 4/0 and so on up to 20/0, which is one of the largest. The length of the hook shank in fractions of an inch, excluding the eye, is used to designate the hook size. But there are some variations in numbering, depending on the style of the hook and, the manufacturer. The safest procedure when ordering hooks is to consult a chart showing, in actual size, ranging from the smallest to the largest, the particular style of hook wanted. Most catalogs showing fishhooks do this. Or you can study the hooks at your tackle dealer's before you buy them.

Hooks also vary in the weight or thickness of the wire used for each size or pattern. Each manufacturer has a standard gauge of wire called "regular" weight for each size of hook. This is his standard weight wire for a particular size and pattern of hook. But hooks are also made of "light" wire, which is thinner in diameter than the standard size wire usually used for that particular size and pattern. Hooks made of light wire are usually labeled 1X fine or 2X fine. The higher the number next to the X, the thinner the wire. Hooks are also made of "heavy" wire, which is a thicker diameter wire than is generally used for a particular size and pattern. Such hooks are labeled 1X stout, 2X stout, or 3X stout. The higher the number next to the X, the thicker the wire.

Before you can select the right hook for the fishing you plan to do, you must take many things into consideration. There is no such thing as an all-around hook suitable for all kinds of fish and fishing. Fish vary widely in the size, shape, and structure of their mouths. They also vary in size, the way they fight on the end of a line, in the way they feed, and in the type of bait or lure they prefer. The size, weight, and pattern of the hook used will also depend on the kind of fishing tackle you will use and where you will fish.

Let's examine some of the more popular patterns of hooks used in fresh and salt-water fishing and find out what kind of fish and fishing they are best suited for. Take the round bend hook, often called the Gaelic Supreme, Viking, or Model Perfect. This hook has a round bend with a large bite and wide gap and a hollow point, allowing deep penetration of the point and barb. It also has excellent holding qualities after a fish is hooked. These hooks are usually made with a turned down eye for fly tying. They are very popular for both dry and wet flies but are also made with a long shank for tying streamer and bucktail flies. This hook can also be used with live baits when a small, sharp, fine-wire hook is required.

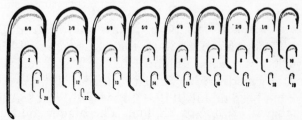

The Mustad Viking-A round bend hook, widely used for tying flies

Another popular hook is the sproat bend, which has been used for many years in fresh and salt water. It is actually a modified round bend hook with a straight point. The sproat is a fine hook when well-made, but it is also turned out with inferior material and poor workmanship for the cheaper markets. It is widely used for bait fishing in fresh and salt water and also for tying large wet flies for bass, salmon, and trout.

The limerick hook is an old Irish design which is still used for the larger fresh-water fish such as bass, walleyes, pike, and muskies. In salt water it is often used for cod and haddock by sport and commercial fishermen. The hook is recognized by its half-round bend, straight point, and heavy wire. The larger wet flies for salmon and trout are often tied on this hook. When made with a long shank, it is widely used for tying streamers and bucktails.

The Aberdeen hook is an excellent pattern for light tackle fishing for small fish when a delicate bait or any natural bait which must kept alive is used. This hook has an almost round bend, wide gap, sharp point, and fine wire. It doesn't injure the bait and leaves a wide gap between the point and hook shank for better hooking. Its light wire enables a live bait to swim or drift naturally in the water and is less visible to the fish. However, because of this thin wire, it should be used only with light tackle and for small fish in fresh and salt water.

In recent years the rolled-in point type of hook such as the well-known "Eagle Claw" made by the Wright & McGill Co. has become very popular. It is one of the most widely used hooks for all kinds of bait fishing in this country. And it is becoming very popular in salt water for use when bait fishing for a wide variety of species. This hook has a rolled-in offset point and is usually made with a ringed or turned down eye. Once this hook has been mouthed by a fish, it is difficult for the fish to get rid of it without getting hooked. These hooks are now made in almost all sizes, finishes, and styles for fresh and salt-water fishing.

The "Eagle Claw" hook made by Wright & McGill Co. is popular for bait fishing

Still another hook for bait fishing is the so-called "big" or "wide-bend" hook. In this hook the gap is very wide, and the bend is curved in toward the shank. This allows the fish to engulf the point and barb well inside the mouth. The point of the hook is also in direct line of pull, giving quick, deep penetration.

The Carlisle pattern has a long shank, making it a good hook for fish which tend to swallow the bait or have sharp teeth. The long shank also makes it useful for hooking and holding such long or large baits as big worms, minnows, and strips of fish.

The Siwash or salmon hook originated in the Pacific Northwest for commercial salmon fishing, but it was quickly adopted by sports anglers for salmon and other fish. East Coast anglers like this hook for striped bass and bluefish. The salmon hook has a round bend, heavy wire, and an extra-long sharp point. It is usually made with a short shank. Since its long, narrow, sharp point will penetrate deeply, this hook is excellent for fish which have tough cartilage mouths. This point also tends to hold leaping fish more securely, allowing less chance for the hook to be thrown.

A highly specialized hook is the Virginia pattern, which is used mostly for blackfish or tautog. The heavy wire and short distance between the point of the hook to the barb make it a strong hook capable of penetrating the tough rubbery lips and withstanding the crushing jaws of this fish.

Another specialized hook is the Chestertown pattern. This hook has a narrow bend, narrow gap, and long shank which fits the sucking, small mouth of the flounder. The long shank helps in removing the hook when it is swallowed. This hook can also be used for catching small eels.

The nearest thing to an all-around hook is the time-favored O'Shaughnessy. This hook has a bend similar to the sproat, but it is usually made of heavier wire. The entire hook is forged or flattened to give it extra strength. In fresh-water fishing it is used for black bass, pike, muskellunge, catfish, sturgeon, and other big fish. In salt water it is very popular for striped bass, channel bass, and bluefish. It is also used for cod, small tuna, bonito, sailfish, white marlin, and all kinds of bottom fish. You'll find the O'Shaughnessy snelled on long and short leaders, molded into metal squids and jigs, attached to spoons, and rigged with baits used in trolling.

In big-game fishing one of the most widely used hooks is the Pfleuger "Sobey," characterized by its extreme round bend, in-point, heavy forged wire construction, and needle eye. It is used mostly for tuna, marlin, swordfish and tarpon. Another Pflueger hook is the "Martu," which has a diamond out-point, insuring quick and deep penetration. It is used for tuna and marlin. The Mustad Company also makes several excellent hooks for big-game fishing. Their "Sea Demon," "Sea Master," "Tarpon and Tuna," and "Giant Tuna" patterns have caught many big fish. Many of the hooks discussed above can also be used when sport fishing for sharks.

The Pflueger Sobey hook, used for large salt-water fish

Some of the largest hooks made are the shark hooks, which are used with heavy lines, mostly by commercial fishermen. These hooks come as long as 12 in. and may have a gap from the point to the shank of 4 or 5 in. They are usually attached to chain leaders from 3 to 6 ft. long.

Then, of course, we have the double and treble hooks, used mostly for artificial lures such as spinners, spoons, and plugs. The small, light-wire treble hooks are usually used for fresh-water fishing. For salt-water you usually need stronger treble hooks made of extra-heavy wire. Big fish can exert a lot of leverage against a treble hook attached to a lure and can straighten them out with surprising ease.

Many anglers buy good hooks and avoid cheap ones because a few cents extra spent on this tiny item of tackle is good insurance. But then many of these same anglers fail to keep their hooks sharp at all times. Even a brand new hook may require touching up at the point. When you're fishing, it always pays to examine your hook to see if the point has dulled, bent, or broken. The lighter the tackle you use, the sharper the hook must be to penetrate the tough mouth of a fish. That is why, when fly fishing, you should always sharpen your point after landing a fish or after hitting the fly against a tree or rock. Even big salt-water hooks require constant touching up to keep them as sharp as possible. For small fresh-water hooks, use a smooth sharpening stone. For larger hooks you can use a coarser carborundum stone or fine file. Always carry this sharpening equipment, and use it often.

It also pays to discard old, rusty hooks which may be dull or weak. It's foolish to take chances with such hooks and then lose a big fish. Replace such hooks with new ones even if it means throwing away a fly or changing the hooks on a lure. It's good insurance; and if you pay more attention to the all-important hook, you're bound to land more and bigger fish in the long run.

21
SINKERS AND WEIGHTS

At one time not too long ago, sinkers and trolling weights were simple, and there weren't too many different kinds to choose from. But today the situation has changed, and the number and variety of sinkers for all methods of fresh and salt-water fishing consists of numerous types and designs. Each type of sinker has specific uses and is best for certain fishing methods and situations.

One of the smallest sinkers used is the round split-shot or BB sinker, which comes in several sizes. These sinkers are split to form a slot wide and deep enough to take a fishing line. They are usually squeezed on with a small pair of pliers and can be removed with a knife blade. The South Bend Co. puts out a special pair of pliers called the "Shot-Master" and discs containing different sizes of split-shot called "Redi-Shot." With this kit you can put the split-shot on a line or leader quickly and remove it easily without damaging the line.

Split-shot sinkers are usually used for fly fishing or in still fishing with baits when only a light weight is needed to get the line or leader down. You can use one, two, or three shot on the leader itself; but if the leader is very thin, care must be taken not to cut or weaken it. Many fly fishermen fishing with worms or other baits like to attach a couple of inches of a dropper nylon to the main leader and add the split-shot to this dropper.

Because split-shot sinkers may damage a fine leader, many fly rod users prefer lead wire, which can be wrapped around their leaders instead. These can be bought in coils of different diameter wire. Somewhat similar are the sheet lead sinkers, which come in narrow strips and are wrapped around a leader or line. These are sold by L. L. Bean Co. of Freeport, Maine, in a matchbook for easy carrying and quick use.

Another sinker commonly used in fresh water and at times in salt water is the clincher sinker, also called the clamp-on or pinch-on sinker. This is the elongated sinker which has on each end ears or folding lugs, which are bent around the line to hold the weight in place. They come in different sizes and weights, from about $\frac{1}{16}$ oz. to an ounce or more. The line is laid in the groove of the sinker; and the ends are folded over, fastening the sinker to the line.

Clincher sinkers in the smaller sizes are used with fly rods or for still fishing to take baits down to certain depths. The larger sizes can be used on the line when trolling shallow water to keep the lure below the surface. The larger sizes are also used in still fishing or when chumming in salt water to take the bait down in a tide or current. Although clincher sinkers are made from very soft lead, care must be taken when putting them on a light leader to make sure that it doesn't get cut or weakened.

Somewhat similar to the clincher sinker in shape is the "Rubbercor" sinker made by the Water Gremlin Co. This sinker also has a slot, but this is lined with rubber and has two rubber tips instead of lead lugs. The line is laid along the sinker slot and against the tips. Then, by pulling the tips slightly and making half turns in opposite directions, the line is held securely.

One of the most popular sinkers used in fresh water for bottom fishing or still fishing is the dipsey or bass-casting sinker. This is the pear-shaped sinker with an eye on the smaller end that swivels or turns. Since they do not tend to twist the line when they roll on the bottom, these sinkers are used frequently in rivers with a current. They come in many sizes and weights, from 1/8 oz. up to 12 or 14 oz. Dipsey sinkers are usually attached to the end of a line, and then a hook on a short leader is tied any distance above the sinker to the main line. The hook is usually baited with some kind of natural bait and is fished on the bottom. These sinkers can also be used for trolling by attaching a short line to the main fishing line and the sinker on the end of the line.

Another sinker often used for bottom fishing is the egg or oval sinker. This sinker is shaped like an egg and has a hole running through the center. The fishing line is run through this hole. Then a small barrel swivel is tied to the end of the line, after which a leader and hook is tied to the remaining eye of the barrel swivel. The barrel swivel acts as a "stop," keeping the sinker from sliding down to the hook. When a fish bites, it can pull line freely through the hole of the sinker without feeling the weight. This sinker is popular in the smaller sizes for carp fishing in fresh water. In salt water it is used in various sizes for all kinds of fish which feed on the bottom. Egg sinkers come in various sizes and weights, from 1/8 oz. up to 10 or 12 oz.

The most popular sinker for salt-water bottom fishing is the "bank" sinker. This is the elongated type sinker with several sides and an eye cast into the head. It is designed to slide through rocks without fouling too quickly. This is the sinker most salt-water anglers fishing on the bottom from boats, piers, bridges, and shore use. The hooks are usually tied above the sinker. Bank sinkers come in many weights, from 1/2 oz. up to a pound or more.

Another salt-water bottom sinker is the diamond-shaped lead. This is a flat sinker used for deep-water fishing and is popular with cod and haddock anglers in northern waters. It comes in the heaviest weights for fishing in deep water on off-shore reefs and banks.

For fishing on bottoms which have many rocks, a round type sinker is used because it doesn't get caught as often as other kinds. This sinker is round like a ball and has an eye on top, to which the line is tied.

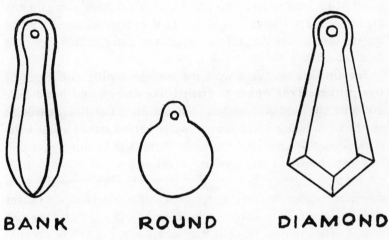

BANK   ROUND   DIAMOND

Common salt-water sinkers

Then we have the pencil sinker which, like its name implies, is long and round like a pencil. It comes in various lengths, diameters, and weights and can be used for bottom fishing or trolling. This type of sinker bounces over rocks when trolled and gets snagged less often than other types.

The pyramid sinker is an old favorite among surf fishermen for bottom fishing along sandy beaches. Shaped like a pyramid with four triangular sides, this sinker digs into the sand and holds bottom in the tide and waves. Pyramid sinkers come in many sizes, with small ones for spinning outfits weighing 1 or 2 oz. and heavier ones running from 3 to 8 oz. The sizes generally used are 4 or 5 oz.

There are also many other kinds of special sinkers which

have peculiar shapes or designs for specific purposes. Some are oval and flat, others are bell shaped, and still others are square. Your local fishing tackle store will usually carry a good assortment of the most popular types of sinkers. Because the price of lead has increased in this Atomic Age, sinkers are more expensive these days. Many anglers who do a lot of fishing find it cheaper to buy a mold and pour their own sinkers. Such molds are also sold in many fishing tackle stores or can be ordered from many mail-order houses which sell fishing tackle or accessories.

For trolling and casting there are many different kinds of weights which can be used. The Pflueger Co. puts out a "Keel-art" sinker which is shaped like a heart when flat. This is folded on the fishing line and acts as a keel to keep the line from twisting. It comes in the lighter weights, from $1/8$ to 1 ounce.

Then there are the trolling keels and weights with bead chains and snaps, which are tied to the line to keep the lure down or to prevent the line from twisting. Keel-shaped swivel weights have a bead chain on both ends and a snap on the tail end. These can also be used for casting lures such as spinners, which tend to twist the line. Or they can be used for trolling. They come in weights from $1/16$ oz. up to 4 oz. for use with various fishing outfits.

Somewhat similar is the elongated lead trolling weight, which also has a bead chain on each end and a snap on the tail end. These come in weights from $1/4$ oz. up to 8 oz. for all kinds of fresh and salt-water trolling. The best way to attach these weights is to tie the weight to the end of the line and then add a nylon leader anywhere from 2 to 8 ft. behind the lead. At the end of the leader you can attach the lure or bait which will be used.

There are also trolling weights of the planing type, which can be adjusted to take the lure down to various depths. One such device is the Luxon Magill stainless steel trolling planer.

It has two planer blades, a lead weight, and seven holes. The trolling depth is pre-selected by setting a pivoting arm in one of the holes. This weight comes in four sizes for both fresh and salt-water trolling.

Most of the trolling weights discussed above are used for shallow waters, with the exception of the planer type, which will take a lure down to 70 fathoms or more. When you are trolling deep, however, such weights can be used with wire line to reach still deeper water.

22

LEADERS, SNAPS AND SWIVELS

This chapter will be devoted to terminal tackle such as leaders, snaps, swivels, and similar connections and items used on the end of the fishing line. We'll start with leaders, which play a vital part in most fresh and salt-water fishing. In fly fishing, for example, the leader serves several functions. First, of course, it makes the fly or lure seem detached from the line and produces more strikes. Second, the leader helps the fly land more delicately on the water. Third, it imparts a more natural movement and action to the fly or lure as it drifts in the current. And a fly leader breaks near the end, saving the rest of the leader and line.

The earlier fly leaders were made from silkworm gut. This natural material left much to be desired. It was brittle when dry and had to be soaked in water before you could tie knots in it or use it for fishing. It was difficult to find natural gut strands longer than 15 in., and even these lengths varied in strength. In the heavier diameters, natural gut is very stiff, wiry, and difficult to tie and handle. Although some natural gut fly leaders are still being sold and used and some anglers use natural gut for tippets, this material is being replaced by the newer synthetic nylon, dacron, and Stren leaders.

When nylon first came out, it was also somewhat stiff and springy. As leader material it was uniform and strong, but in

200

the thinner diameters it wasn't quite limp enough. In recent years, however, great improvements have been made in producing limp nylon. Today nylon leaders are used by the great majority of fly fishermen.

Another good leader material is platyl, which is limp, uniform, and thin in diameter for its strength. It is available in many diameters for tying all kinds of fly leaders. It is very popular for tippets and comes in small plastic dispensers, which hold a coil of this material.

In recent years leaders made from the Du Pont material Stren have also been used for fly fishing. This material is limp, strong, and very thin in diameter for any given pound test. Its gun-metal gray color makes it almost invisible.

The simplest fly leader is a level leader which is of the same diameter for its entire length. Such leaders are occasionally used today for bait fishing and for casting streamers, bucktails, spinners, or other heavy fly rod lures. But for use with dry flies, wet flies, and nymphs, the tapered leader is the choice of most fly fishermen.

Tapered leaders step down in diameter from the butt or thickest part to the tippet or thinnest part. In a knotted tapered leader this graduation consists of several strands of leader material of different diameters tied together. A knotless leader is drawn in a single strand and graduates evenly from the thickest to the thinnest part without the use of knots. Both types of leaders can be bought already made up in almost any fishing tackle store.

Commercially tied fly leaders usually come in 7½ and 9 ft. lengths for most fly fishing in fresh and salt water. The diameter of the thin end or tippet is indicated as 0x, 1x, 2x, 3x, 4x, and so on down to 7x, which is one of the thinnest. The diameter of the tippet and butt ends is also indicated in 1000ths inch and the breaking test.

Many fly leaders sold over the counter are not perfect for a given angler, his fishing tackle, and the fishing he plans to do. Some anglers like to use longer leaders, up to 12 or even 15 ft. Many commercial leaders also have butt ends which are too light and require the addition of one or two lengths of heavier leader material. So many fly fishermen prefer to tie their own fly leaders and buy nylon, platyl, or Stren leader material in coils for this purpose.

It requires considerable experimenting to find the right length, diameter, and taper of a particular leader for a given angler, rod, and fishing conditions. The choice of a fly leader will depend on many factors such as the angler's style of casting, the type of water being fished, the bulk of the fly or lure, the condition of the water, wind, and so forth.

On narrow streams, for example, and for casting with short rods, the shorter fly leaders are used. On big waters and for use with the longer rods, you can use the longer leaders. For dry-fly fishing you'll need finer and thinner leaders than when fishing with wet flies, streamers, bucktails, or bass bugs. For wary fish and clear, low, placid waters, you'll also need finer leaders. When the water is rough or slightly clouded, you can use heavier leaders. Small fish can be landed on lighter leaders than the bigger fish. And naturally, the leaders used for bass, steelhead, salmon, and salt-water fish will be heavier than those used for trout.

The thin lines used in spin fishing are a great advantage when it comes to casting. You get plenty of distance even with light lures, and the lines play an important part in fooling wary fish. Yet these same lines offer a disadvantage when it comes to the wear and tear on the first few feet. Constant casting of lures often weakens the line where it rubs against the tip guide; and if too heavy a lure is used, the shock of casting may break the line. The thin lines also can't take much rubbing against rocks, logs, coral, mussels, barnacles, and weeds. Then there's the strain of landing or boating a fish from shore or a boat.

You may have to hold the fish from running under the boat or around the motor, or you may have to partially drag the fish in shallow water or on the ground. In some spots you may even have to lift a small fish a short distance. In surf fishing you have to fight the current, surf, and waves when beaching a fish. Then there are fish with sharp teeth, gill plates, or fins, which can quickly sever a thin line. Or you may get hung up in a branch, weeds, or the bottom and have to pull free.

All these thing add up to wear and tear on thin spinning lines; so anglers use various kinds of leaders to take some of the strain and wear off the lines. In fishing fresh waters such as trout streams where there are clear, open waters and no obstructions, leaders may be unnecessary. In this case a leader may cut down on the strikes you get when you use a spinning outfit.

But in most fishing situations a shock leader in front of the main fishing line will save fish and lures. If you do require a leader when spinning, the simplest one to use is another piece of nylon monofilament a few pounds stronger than your main line. For best results such a leader should be long enough so that when your lure is ready to cast, a few turns of the leaders are on the reel spool. This is especialy important in salt-water spinning, where heavy lures will break light lines and tend to cut your index finger. The length of your leader will depend on the length of your rod and the distance your lure hangs from the rod tip. It will vary; but as long as you have a few turns of your leader on your reel spool, the strain is off your line. This if you are using 4 lb. test nylon monofilament or other mono line, you can use a leader of the same material testing 6 lb. If your are surf fishing with 15 lb. test line, you can use a leader testing 20 lb., and so on.

For bait-casting outfits a nylon or other mono leader is almost a must if you are using braided line. This line is readily seen in clear water, and you'll get more strikes if you attach a monofilament leader ahead of the line. This can be the same pound test as the braided line. A leader about 4 to 6 ft. long will usually be long enough for this. Of course, if you are using monofilament line on your casting reel, a leader is not vital unless you want to add a leader heavier than your line when fishing around obstructions.

Surf anglers fishing with conventional rods and reels also use braided nylon or squidding line. This, too, is highly visible in clear water although when the surf is rough it doesn't matter too much. But in clear water you'll get more strikes if you add a nylon monofilament leader about 6 to 8 ft. long ahead of your line.

There are several knots which can be used to attach the leader to the line, but the most widely used is the blood knot. Another way is to make an end loop on the leader and another loop on the end of the line and interlock them. Other knots used for monofilament leader material of line are the improved clinch knot and the improved end loop knot. These are shown in drawings here as recommended by the Du Pont Co., which has found, after many studies, that when tying the improved clinch knot or the blood knot at least five turns should be made around the standing part of the line.

Wire leaders are not often required in fresh-water fishing except when you're going after such species as pike and muskellunge. Then a short wire leader of several inches can often be used. But in salt-water fishing you often need wire leaders on your lures or hooks, not only because of such sharp-toothed fish as bluefish and barracuda, but because fins and gill covers of many salt-water fish will quickly cut an ordinary nylon leader or line.

Such wire leaders will vary with the type of fish you are seeking and the fishing you are doing. Small, short leaders are often permanently attached to jigs, metal squids, plugs, and other lures especially for casting or surf fishing. These are often no more than 6 to 8 in. long. One end has a small loop or eye, to which the snap on the line or leader is attached. The other end of the wire leader is permanently attached to the lure with a big loop to permit the lure to have plenty of action.

For trolling in salt water for the smaller fish such as bluefish, striped bass, channel bass, albacore, bonito, and barracuda, you can use wire leaders anywhere from 3 to 10 ft. long.

For trolling, still fishing, or drift fishing offshore for the larger gamefish, leaders may run anywhere from 15 to 30 ft. long. The line, too, may be doubled as a safety measure.

Two kinds of wire leaders are usually used for salt-water fishing. One is the cable type leader, usually made from stainless steel. The cable wire comes bare or is covered with nylon or other plastic. To make loops for attaching snaps, swivels, and hooks to this cable wire, it must be crimped with special crimping or swaging pliers. A small brass or copper sleeve or tube is used. The end of the cable leader is passed through the sleeve until it protrudes about an inch and a half on the other side. Then the end of the cable wire is doubled back through the sleeve, forming a loop. The sleeve is then pinched with the special crimping pliers. The crimping pliers, sleeves, and wire are sold by the Berkley Co. in a handy leader crimping kit. They call their cable leader material "Steelon." Pliers and kits can be bought in many tackle stores. For very large fish such as swordfish, giant tuna, and marlin, the cable wire leaders with hook attached can be bought in tackle stores.

The other wire leader material is the single strand stainless steel which comes in large coils. There are two types, the shiny kind and the dull finish. In surf fishing it doesn't make much difference which kind you use. But for trolling or bait fishing in clear water, the non-shiny leaders are best. This wire leader material comes in coils in various pound tests, with No. 5 testing about 44 lb. and No. 18, one of the heaviest diameters, testing 325 lb. To make your own leaders with this wire, you need a pair of side-cutting pliers, flat-nosed gripping pliers, and round-nosed pliers.

Various kinds of snaps, swivels, and similar connections are required at times in fresh and salt-water fishing. When fishing trout streams or clear lakes with wary fish, it is often best to tie the leader directly to the lure. The same thing holds true when fishing for bonefish and for bonito or albacore with small lures. However, if you plan to use many different kinds of lures for other fish, you can waste a lot of time cutting off the lures and then tying on new ones. Most anglers use some kind of snap or snap-swivel for changing lures quickly. When casting or trolling with lures which spin, a swivel also helps to keep the line from twisting.

Barrel swivels come in various sizes for fresh and salt-water fishing, from the largest, No. 6/0, which tests from 300 to 500 lb. and is used for big-game fish, to the smallest, the No. 12, which tests from 20 to 40 lb. and is used for small fish. Barrel swivels come with twisted wire loops, plain wire eyes, and with ball-bearings such as the "Sampo" swivel. This has rings on

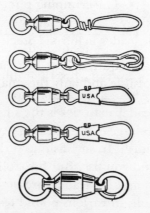

The Sampo ball bearing swivel and different types of snaps it is used with

each end and ball bearings inside the body. You can get swivels in plain brass, chrome-plated, or dull black finishes.

There are also three-way swivels, which come in various sizes and have a three-point attachment with eyes for the line, sinker, and leader with hook. They are popular with surf anglers and bottom fishermen. Somewhat similar is the cross-line swivel with a barrel swivel and locking snaps for quick changing of rigs or leaders.

Snap-swivels also come in different types for the quick-changing of lures. Most of them have a barrel swivel on one end and a locking or safety snap on the other. In recent years many of these snaps have been made with round loops which permit a lure to work freely without hindering its action. There are many sizes and strengths of snap-swivels for fresh and salt-water fishing. One of the best snaps or snap-swivels made of stainless steel is the one designed by Ed Hatch of Pompanette Products. It is extremely strong and dependable in all the different sizes. Other good snaps and swivels are the Kelux and Luxon products by the Art Wire and Stamping Co. The Bead Chain Mfg. Co. makes some excellent snap-swivels of the bead chain type.

Actually, snaps, swivels and other terminal hardware are invaluable when they are needed to do a particular job. When you have to use them, do so; but don't add more than you need or use larger sizes than required. The best rule is to use as few snaps or swivels as possible and only the smallest sizes that are practical.

INDEX